Microsoft® Word 2016

Nita Rutkosky
Pierce College at Puyallup
Puyallup, Washington

Audrey Roggenkamp
Pierce College at Puyallup
Puyallup, Washington

Ian Rutkosky
Pierce College at Puyallup
Puyallup, Washington

PARADIGM
EDUCATION SOLUTIONS
St. Paul

Senior Vice President	Linda Hein
Editor in Chief	Christine Hurney
Director of Production	Timothy W. Larson
Production Editors	Rachel Kats, Jen Weaverling
Cover and Text Designer	Valerie King
Copy Editor	Sarah Kearin
Senior Design and Production Specialist	Jaana Bykonich
Assistant Developmental Editors	Mamie Clark, Katie Werdick
Testers	Desiree Carvel; Ann E. Mills, Ivy Tech Community College of Indiana, Indianapolis, IN
Instructional Support Writer	Brienna McWade
Indexer	Terry Casey
Vice President Information Technology	Chuck Bratton
Digital Projects Manager	Tom Modl
Vice President Sales and Marketing	Scott Burns
Director of Marketing	Lara Weber McLellan

Care has been taken to verify the accuracy of information presented in this book. However, the authors, editors, and publisher cannot accept responsibility for Web, email, newsgroup, or chat room subject matter or content, or for consequences from application of the information in this book, and make no warranty, expressed or implied, with respect to its content.

Trademarks: Microsoft is a trademark or registered trademark of Microsoft Corporation in the United States and/or other countries. Some of the product names and company names included in this book have been used for identification purposes only and may be trademarks or registered trade names of their respective manufacturers and sellers. The authors, editors, and publisher disclaim any affiliation, association, or connection with, or sponsorship or endorsement by, such owners.

Cover Photo Credits: © whitehoune/Shutterstock.com; © Mila Supinskaya/Shutterstock.com.

We have made every effort to trace the ownership of all copyrighted material and to secure permission from copyright holders. In the event of any question arising as to the use of any material, we will be pleased to make the necessary corrections in future printings. Thanks are due to the aforementioned authors, publishers, and agents for permission to use the materials indicated.

ISBN 978-0-76486-699-0 (text)
ISBN 978-0-76386-700-3 (digital)

© 2017 by Paradigm Publishing, Inc.
875 Montreal Way
St. Paul, MN 55102
Email: educate@emcp.com
Website: ParadigmCollege.com

Printed in the United States of America

24 23 22 21 20 19 18 17 16   1 2 3 4 5 6 7 8 9 10

Contents

Word 2016

Microsoft Word 2016 is a word processing program used to create documents such as letters, reports, research papers, brochures, announcements, newsletters, envelopes, labels, and much more. Word is a full-featured program that provides a wide variety of editing and formatting features as well as sophisticated visual elements. While working in Word, you will produce business documents for the following six companies.

First Choice Travel is a travel center offering a full range of traveling services from booking flights, hotel reservations, and rental cars to offering travel seminars.

The Waterfront Bistro offers fine dining for lunch and dinner and also offers banquet facilities, a wine cellar, and catering services.

Worldwide Enterprises is a national and international distributor of products for a variety of companies and is the exclusive movie distribution agent for Marquee Productions.

Marquee Productions is involved in all aspects of creating movies from script writing and development to filming. The company produces documentaries, biographies, as well as historical and action movies.

Performance Threads maintains an inventory of rental costumes and also researches, designs, and sews special-order and custom-made costumes.

The mission of the Niagara Peninsula College Theatre Arts Division is to offer a curriculum designed to provide students with a thorough exposure to all aspects of the theatre arts.

In Section 1 you will learn how to

Create and Edit Documents

Use Microsoft Word to create, edit, and format a variety of business documents and use Word's powerful editing and formatting features to produce well-written and visually appealing documents. Some powerful editing features include checking the spelling and grammar in a document and using Thesaurus to find appropriate synonyms for words; using AutoCorrect to improve the efficiency of entering information in a document; and creating a document using a predesigned template.

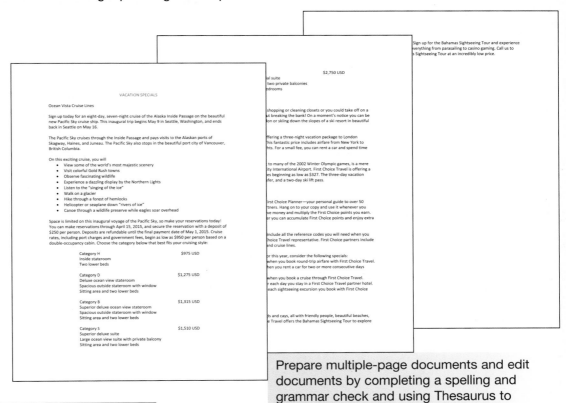

VACATION SPECIALS

Ocean Vista Cruise Lines

Sign up today for an eight-day, seven-night cruise of the Alaska Inside Passage on the beautiful new Pacific Sky cruise ship. This inaugural trip begins May 9 in Seattle, Washington, and ends back in Seattle on May 16.

The Pacific Sky cruises through the Inside Passage and pays visits to the Alaskan ports of Skagway, Haines, and Juneau. The Pacific Sky also stops in the beautiful port city of Vancouver, British Columbia.

On this exciting cruise, you will
- View some of the world's most majestic scenery
- Visit colorful Gold Rush towns
- Observe fascinating wildlife
- Experience a dazzling display by the Northern Lights
- Listen to the "singing of the ice"
- Walk on a glacier
- Hike through a forest of hemlocks
- Helicopter or seaplane down "rivers of ice"
- Canoe through a wildlife preserve while eagles soar overhead

Space is limited on this inaugural voyage of the Pacific Sky, so make your reservations today! You can make reservations through April 15, 2015, and secure the reservation with a deposit of $250 per person. Deposits are refundable until the final payment date of May 1, 2015. Cruise rates, including port charges and government fees, begin as low as $950 per person based on a double-occupancy cabin. Choose the category below that best fits your cruising style:

Category H Inside stateroom Two lower beds	$975 USD
Category D Deluxe ocean view stateroom Spacious outside stateroom with window Sitting area and two lower beds	$1,275 USD
Category B Superior deluxe ocean view stateroom Spacious outside stateroom with window Sitting area and two lower beds	$1,315 USD
Category S Superior deluxe suite Large ocean view suite with private balcony Sitting area and two lower beds	$1,510 USD

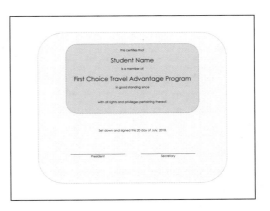

Prepare multiple-page documents and edit documents by completing a spelling and grammar check and using Thesaurus to find appropriate synonyms for words.

7/20/2018

Student Name
Marquee Productions
955 South Alameda Street
Los Angeles, CA 90017

Ms. Melissa Gehring
First Choice Travel
3588 Ventura Boulevard
Los Angeles, CA 90102

Dear Ms. Gehring:

Marquee Productions will be filming a movie in and around the Toronto area from July 9 through August 31, 2018. I would like scheduling and pricing information for flights from Los Angeles to Toronto, as well as information on lodging.

Approximately 45 people from our company will need flight reservations and hotel rooms. Please locate the best group rates and let me know the approximate costs. I would like to finalize preparations by the end of the month.

Sincerely,

Student Name
Projects Coordinator
Marquee Productions

This certifies that

Student Name

is a member of

First Choice Travel Advantage Program

in good standing since

with all rights and privileges pertaining thereof.

Set down and signed this 20 day of July, 2018.

_____   _____
President   Secretary

Download online templates from and create a variety of documents including letters, faxes, certificates, or awards.

In Section 2 you will learn how to

Format Characters and Paragraphs in Documents

Word contains a number of commands and procedures that affect how the document appears when printed. The appearance of a document in the document screen and how it looks when printed is called the *format*. Formatting can include such tasks as changing the font; aligning and indenting text; changing line and paragraph spacing; setting tabs; and inserting elements such as bullets, numbers, symbols, and special characters. The readability of a document can be improved by setting text in tabbed columns and by formatting using styles.

Apply font formatting such as changing the font, font size, and font color. Apply paragraph formatting such as changing alignment, indentations, and line spacing.

Apply formatting such as inserting bullets and special characters, setting text in tabbed columns, applying paragraph shading and lines, and inserting a page border. Use style sets to apply predesigned formatting such as bolding and centering text, changing fonts, and applying border lines to headings.

In Section 3 you will learn how to

Enhance Documents

Improve the formatting of a document using features to rearrange text in a document, add special elements, or change the appearance of text. Use buttons on the Home tab to move, copy, and paste text in a document. Improve the appearance of documents by inserting page numbering, headers, and footers; changing margins and page orientation; and changing vertical alignment. Add visual appeal to documents by inserting and customizing images.

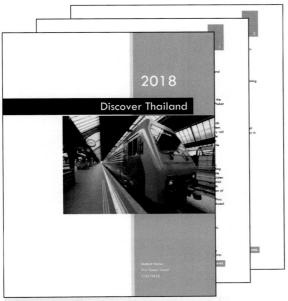

Enhance the visual appeal of a document by inserting an image related to text in the document, and a page border and background color.

Enhance the appearance of a document by applying a theme, which is a set of formatting choices that includes a color, a font, and effects; inserting a cover page; inserting a watermark, which is a lightened image that displays behind text; and inserting a header and footer.

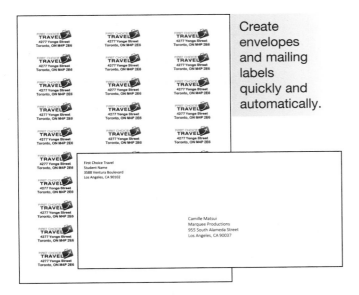

Create envelopes and mailing labels quickly and automatically.

Format a research paper or report in the MLA (Modern Language Association) style.

In Section 4 you will learn how to

Apply Special Features

Word contains special formatting features that can be applied to a document to enhance the visual display of text. For example, add visual appeal to a document with the WordArt and drop cap features and by inserting shapes. Use the SmartArt feature to create visual representations of data such as organizational charts and graphics, and use the Tables feature to create, modify, and format data in columns and rows. Improve the ease with which others can read and understand text by setting it in columns. Insert hyperlinks in a Word document that will link to another file or a location on the Internet and save a Word document in the PDF file format.

Use Word's special features to enhance a document with WordArt text, a drop cap, and a built-in text box. Improve the readability of a document by setting text in columns.

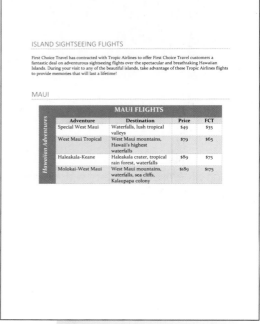

Insert columnar data in a table and format the table to make the data easier to read and understand.

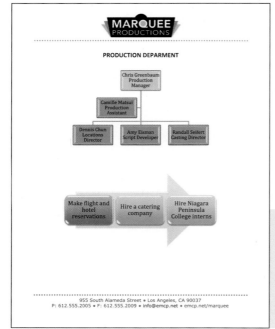

Use Word's SmartArt feature to illustrate hierarchical data in an organizational chart or create a graphic to show data processes, cycles, or relationships or present data in a matrix or pyramid.

Getting Started

Adjusting Monitor Settings, Copying Data Files, and Changing View Options

Skills

- Set monitor resolution
- Modify DPI settings
- Copy files from OneDrive

- Copy files from a network location
- Change view options
- Display file extensions

The Microsoft Office product line has evolved over time, becoming available on Apple computers, tablets, phones, and through the Internet. This textbook and the accompanying ebook were written using a typical personal computer (tower/box, monitor, keyboard and mouse) or laptop. While you may be able to perform some of the activities in this textbook on a different operating system or tablet, not all of the steps will work as written and may jeopardize any work you may be required to turn in to your instructor. If you do not have access to a compatible computer, explore what options you have at your institution such as where and when you can use a computer lab.

One of the evolutions of the Microsoft Office product is that it is now offered in a subscription-based plan called Microsoft Office 365. An advantage of having a Microsoft Office 365 subscription is that it includes and incorporates new features or versions as they are released, as long as your subscription is active. For example, when Microsoft released Office 2016, any Office 365 users with the Office 2013 version were automatically upgraded. This new direction Microsoft is taking may impact section activities and assessments. For example, new features and tweaks may alter how some of the steps are completed. The ebook will contain the most up-to-date material and will be updated as new features become available.

In Activity 1 you will customize your monitor settings so that what you see on the screen matches the images in this textbook. In Activity 2 you will obtain the data files you will be using throughout this textbook from OneDrive. Activity 3 includes instructions on how to change the view settings so that your view of files in a FIle Explorer window matches the images in this textbook.

Activity 1 Adjusting Monitor Settings

Before beginning projects in this textbook, you may need to customize your monitor's settings and turn on the display of file extensions. Projects in the sections in this textbook assume that the monitor display is set at 1600 x 900 pixels, the DPI is set at 125%, and that the display of file extensions is turned on. Adjusting a monitor's display settings is important because the ribbon in the Microsoft Office applications adjusts to the screen resolution setting of your computer monitor. A monitor set at a high resolution will have the ability to show more buttons in the ribbon than a monitor set to a low resolution. The illustrations in this textbook were created with a screen resolution display set at 1600 × 900 pixels. In Figure GS1 at the bottom of the page, the Word ribbon is shown three ways: at a lower screen resolution (1366 × 768 pixels), at the screen resolution featured throughout this textbook, and at a higher screen resolution (1920 × 1080 pixels). Note the variances in the ribbon in all three examples.

What You Will Do Adjust the monitor settings for your machine to match the settings used to create the images in the textbook. If using a lab computer, check with your instructor before attempting this activity.

1 Right-click a blank area of the desktop and then click the *Display settings* option at the shortcut menu.

2 At the Settings window with the *Display* option selected, scroll down and click the <u>Advanced display settings</u> hyperlink.

3 Scroll down and look at the current setting displayed in the *Resolution* option box. For example, your screen may be currently set at 1920 × 1080. If your screen is already set to 1600 × 900, skip ahead to Step 7.

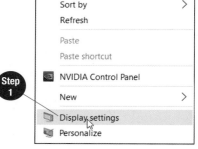

> Screen resolution is set in pixels. Pixel is the abbreviation of picture element and refers to a single dot or point on the display monitor. Changing the screen resolution to a higher number of pixels means that more information can be seen on the screen as items are scaled to a smaller size.

Figure GS1 Word Ribbon at Various Screen Resolutions

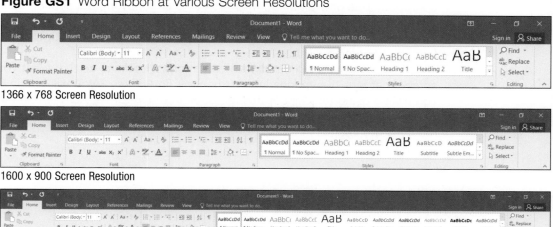

1366 x 768 Screen Resolution

1600 x 900 Screen Resolution

1920 x 1080 Screen Resolution

4 Click the *Resolution* option box and then click the 1600 × 900 option. If necessary, check with your instructor for alternate instructions. ***Note: Depending on the privileges you are given on a school machine, you may not be able to complete these steps.***

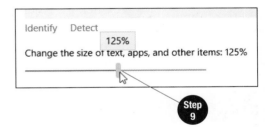

> If the machine you are using has more than one monitor, make sure the proper monitor is selected. (The active monitor displays as a blue rectangle.)

5 Click the Apply button.

6 Click the Keep changes button at the message box asking if you want to keep the display settings.

> Some monitor settings will render the computer unusable because objects on the desktop or in a window will become inaccessible and hidden. In this case, Windows will automatically revert the settings to the previous configuration after 30 seconds.

7 Click the Back button.

8 At the Settings window with the *Display* option active, look at the percentage in which the size of text, apps, and other items currently display (also known as the DPI setting). For example, items on your screen may display at 100%. If the percentage is 125%, skip to Step 12.

> As the resolution on monitors has increased, text, application windows, buttons, options, and so on start to appear smaller and smaller on the screen. To counter this, Windows allows you to increase the size of these objects by changing the DPI setting. The computers used to create the images in this textbook uses the 125% DPI setting, which slightly increases the size of text, applications, buttons, and options.

9 Click and hold down the left mouse button on the button on the slider bar below the text *Change the size of text, apps, and other items*, drag the slider button until *125%* displays, and then release the mouse button.

10 Click the Apply button.

11 At the message indicating that you must sign out of your computer, click the Sign out later button.

12 Click the Close button.

Activity 2   Retrieving and Copying Data Files

While working through the activities in this book, you will often be using data files as starting points. These files need to be obtained from OneDrive or other locations such as your school's network drive. All of the files required to complete the bookwork are provided through OneDrive, which you can access through links in the textbook's ebook. Make sure you have Internet access before trying to retrieve the data files from OneDrive. Ask your instructor if alternate locations are available for retrieving the files, such as a network drive or online resource such as Angel, BlackBoard, or Canvas. Retrieving data files from an alternate location will require different steps, so check with your instructor for additional steps or tasks to complete.

What You Will Do   In order to complete the activities in this textbook, you will need to obtain the data files from OneDrive. Make sure you have access to OneDrive or an alternate location containing the files.

1 Insert your USB flash drive into an available USB port.

2 Navigate to this textbook's ebook. If you are a SNAP user, navigate to the ebook by clicking the textbook ebook link on your Assignments page. If you are not a SNAP user, launch your browser, go to https://paradigm.bookshelf.emcp.com, log in, and then click the textbook ebook thumbnail. *Note: The steps in this activity assume you are using the Microsoft Edge browser. If you are using a different browser, the following steps may vary.*

3 Navigate to the ebook page that corresponds to this textbook page.

4 Click the Ancillary Links button in the menu. The menu of buttons may be at the top of the window or along the side of the window, depending on the size of the window.

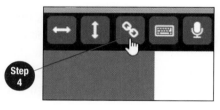

Data Files ▶ **5** At the Ancillary Links dialog box that appears, click the <u>Data Files: All Files</u> hyperlink.

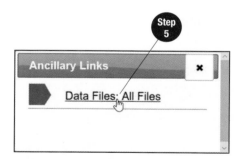

6 Click the <u>Download</u> hyperlink at the top of the window.

A zip file containing the student data files will automatically begin downloading from the OneDrive website.

7 Click the Open button in the message box saying that the DataFiles.zip has finished downloading.

8 Right-click the *ExcelS2* folder in the Content pane.

9 Click the *Copy* option at the shortcut menu.

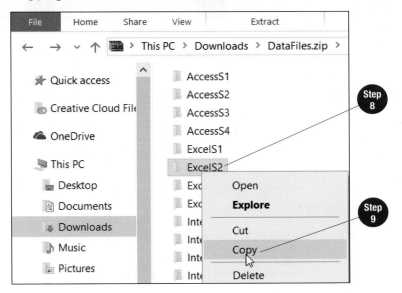

10 Click your USB flash drive that displays in the Navigation pane at the left side of the File Explorer window.

11 Click the Home tab and then click the Paste button in the Clipboard group.

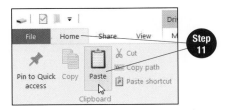

12 Close the File Explorer window by clicking the Close button in the upper right corner of the window.

Activity 3   Changing View Options

You can change the view of the File Explorer window to show the contents of your current location (drive or folder) in various formats, including icons, tiles, or a list, among others. With the Content pane in Details view, you can click the column headings to change how the contents are sorted and whether they are sorted in ascending or descending order. You can customize a window's environment by using buttons and options on the File Explorer View tab. You can also change how panes are displayed, how content is arranged in the Content pane, how content is sorted, and which features are hidden.

What You Will Do   Before getting started with the textbook material, you need to adjust the view settings so that items in the File Explorer window appear the same as the images in the textbook.

1 Click the File Explorer button on the taskbar.

> By default, a File Explorer window opens at the Quick access location, which contains frequently-used folders such as Desktop, Documents, Downloads, Pictures and so on. It also displays recently used files at the bottom of the Content pane.

2 Click the drive letter representing your storage medium in the Navigation pane.

3 Double-click the *ExcelS2* folder in the Content pane.

4 Click the View tab below the Title bar.

5 Click the *Large icons* option in the Layout group.

> After you click an option on the View tab, the View tab collapses to provide more space in the File Explorer window.

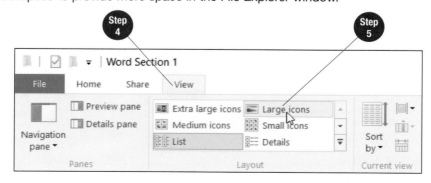

6 Click the View tab.

7 Click the *Details* option in the Layout group.

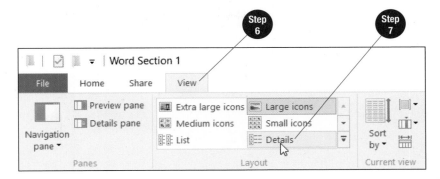

8 With files now displayed in Details view, click the *Name* column heading to sort the list in descending order by name.

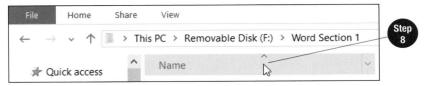

9 Click the *Name* column heading again to restore the list to ascending order by name.

10 Click the View tab and then click the *File name extensions* check box in the Show/hide group to insert a check mark. ***Note: If the check box appears with a check mark in it, then file extensions are already turned on—skip this step.***

Inserting a check mark in a check box makes the option active. The files in the File Explorer window will now display any files with a file extension.

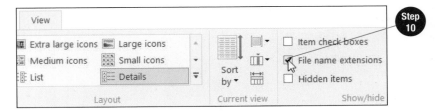

11 Close the File Explorer window by clicking the Close button in the upper right corner of the window.

In Addition

Changing the Default View for All Folders

You can set a view to display by default for all folders of a similar type (such as all disk drive folders or all documents folders). To do this, change the current view to the desired view for the type of folder that you want to set. Next, click the Options button on the View tab and then click the View tab at the Folder Options dialog box. Click the Apply to Folders button in the Folder views section and then click OK. Click Yes at the Folder Views message asking if you want all folders of this type to match this folder's view settings.

Word

Creating and Editing a Document

Data Files ▶ Before beginning section work, copy the WordS1 folder to your storage medium and then make WordS1 the active folder.

Skills

- Create, save, and print a document
- Close a document and close Word
- Move the insertion point
- Insert and delete text
- Scroll in a document
- Select, replace, and delete text
- Use Undo and Redo
- Check the spelling and grammar in a document
- Use AutoCorrect
- Use the Thesaurus
- Change document views
- Hide and show white space

- Change the display percentage
- Navigate and find text using the Navigation pane
- Find and replace text
- Use the Tell Me feature
- Use the Help feature
- Review and print a document
- Create a document using a template
- Create, rename, and delete a folder
- Copy and paste a document
- Save a document in a different format

Precheck ▶ Check your current skills to help focus your study of the skills taught in this section.

Projects Overview

 Prepare a document describing a special vacation package and edit and format two documents describing various vacation specials offered by First Choice Travel.

 Customize a sample employee incentive agreement and prepare a fax cover page for the agreement.

 Use a letter template to prepare one letter to First Choice Travel regarding a movie site and another to the manager of The Waterfront Bistro requesting catering information.

 Edit a letter to Marquee Productions regarding costuming for a film.

 Write a letter to Josh Hart at Marquee Productions explaining the catering services offered by The Waterfront Bistro and then prepare a fax sheet for the letter.

 **SNAP** If you are a SNAP user, launch the Precheck and Tutorials from your Assignments page.

Model Answers ▶ Preview the model answers for an overview of the projects you will complete in the section activities.

1

Microsoft Word is a word processing program you can use to create, save, edit, and print documents. To create a document in Word, open the Word program and then click the *Blank document* template. This opens a blank document with the insertion point positioned at the beginning of the document. The document screen contains a variety of features for working with a document, such as the Title bar, Quick Access Toolbar, ribbon, and Status bar. Type text in a document and press the Enter key, and the insertion point moves down to the next line with extra spacing above the line. If you want to create a new line without including the extra spacing, use the New Line command: Shift + Enter. When entering text, Word includes an AutoCorrect feature that will automatically correct certain words that are entered incorrectly. After creating a document, save the document so it is available for future use. Save a document at the Save As dialog box.

What You Will Do As an employee of First Choice Travel, you have been asked to create a short document containing information on a travel package. You will save and then print the document so you can send it to other employees for review.

Tutorial
Opening a Blank Document

Tutorial
Exploring the Word Screen

Tutorial
Entering Text

Tutorial
Undoing an AutoCorrect Correction

Tutorial
Saving with a New Name

Tutorial
Printing a Document

1 At the Windows 10 desktop, click the Start button and then click the Word 2016 tile.

Depending on your system configuration, these steps may vary.

2 At the Word 2016 opening screen, click the *Blank document* template.

3 At the blank Word document, identify the various features by comparing your screen with the one shown in Figure 1.1.

Refer to Table 1.1 for a description of the screen features.

Figure 1.1 Word Document Screen

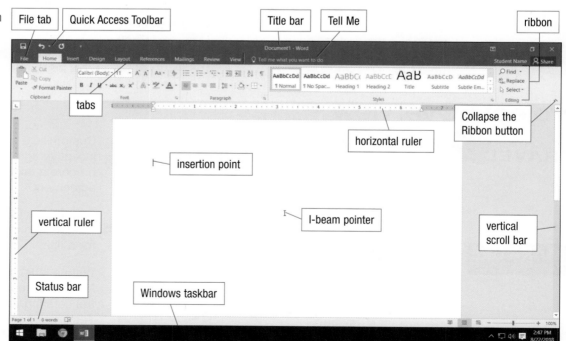

Table 1.1 Screen Features and Descriptions

Feature	Description
Collapse the Ribbon button	when clicked, removes the ribbon from the screen (redisplay the ribbon by clicking a tab [except the File tab] and then clicking the Pin the ribbon button [previously the Collapse the Ribbon button)
File tab	when clicked, displays the backstage area that contains options for working with and managing documents
horizontal ruler	used to set margins, indents, and tabs
I-beam pointer	used to move the insertion point or to select text
insertion point	indicates location of next character entered at the keyboard
Quick Access Toolbar	contains buttons for commonly used commands
ribbon	area containing tabs with options and buttons divided into groups
Status bar	displays number of pages and words, view buttons, and Zoom slider bar
tabs	contain commands and buttons organized into groups
Tell Me	used to look up a feature and provide options for using the feature
Title bar	displays document name followed by program name
vertical ruler	used to set top and bottom margins
vertical scroll bar	used to view various parts of the document beyond the screen
Windows taskbar	divided into three sections—the Start button, the task buttons area, and the notification area

4 Type Moment's Notice Travel Package as shown in Figure 1.2 and then press the Enter key.

> Pressing the Enter key begins a new paragraph in the document.

5 Type First Choice Travel, hold down the Shift key, press the Enter key, and then release the Shift key.

> Shift + Enter is the New Line command. Use this command to keep lines of text within the same paragraph, which creates less space between one line and the next.

6 Type Los Angeles Office and then press the Enter key.

7 Type the remainder of the text shown in Figure 1.2.

> Type the text as shown. When you type *adn* and then press the spacebar, the AutoCorrect feature will automatically correct it to *and*. When you type *teh* and then press the spacebar, AutoCorrect corrects it to *the*. Do not press the Enter key to end a line of text within a paragraph. Word will automatically wrap text to the next line.

8 Click the File tab to display the backstage area.

> The File tab is located in the upper left corner of the screen at the left side of the Home tab.

Figure 1.2 Steps 4–7

Moment's Notice Travel Package

First Choice Travel
Los Angeles Office

Are you spontaneous adn enjoy doing something on a moment's notice? If this describes you, then you will be interested in the First Choice Travel Moment's Notice Travel Package. For teh low price of $599 you can fly from New York to London for a four-day stay. The catch to this incredible deal is that you must make your reservation within the next week and complete your London stay within 30 days.

9 Click the *Save As* option.

10 At the Save As backstage area, click the *Browse* option.

If you are saving to your OneDrive, click the *OneDrive - Personal* option. Click the desired folder in the right panel, click in the *File name* text box at the Save As dialog box, type the desired document name, and then press the Enter key.

11 At the Save As dialog box, click the drive in the Navigation pane that contains your storage medium.

Press the F12 function key to display the Save As dialog box without displaying the Save As backstage area.

12 Double-click the *WordS1* folder in the Content pane.

13 Click in the *File name* text box, type 1-FCTTravelPkg, and then press the Enter key (or click the Save button).

Word automatically adds the file extension *.docx* to the end of a document name.

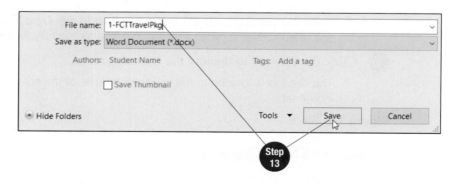

14 Print the document by clicking the File tab, clicking the *Print* option, and then clicking the Print button at the Print backstage area.

When you click the File tab, the backstage area displays with options for working with and managing documents. Refer to Table 1.2 for descriptions of the options and information you will find in each option's backstage area.

**Save Document
to Removable Disk**
1. Press F12.
2. In Navigation pane at
   Save As dialog box,
   click drive containing
   removable disk.
3. Double-click folder in
   Content pane.
4. Click in *File name* text
   box.
5. Type document name.
6. Press Enter.

Print Document
1. Click File tab.
2. Click *Print* option.
3. Click Print button.

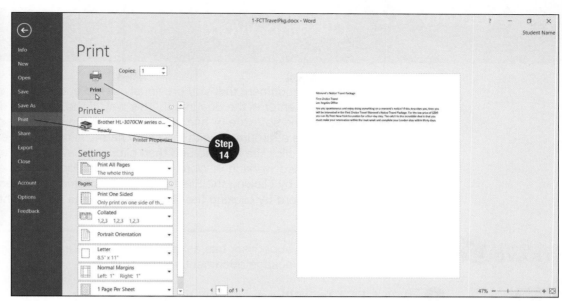

Table 1.2 Backstage Area Options

Option	Information
Info	permissions, possible issues with sharing the document, document versions, properties (for example, number of pages, number of words), date created, date last modified, date last printed, author
New	available templates such as Blank document as well as online templates
Open	options for opening documents; list of recently opened documents
Save	saves previously saved document or displays Save As backstage area with options and locations for saving a document
Save As	options and locations for saving a document
Print	number of copies, printer, settings (for example, one-sided pages, letter size, normal margins, one page per sheet)
Share	share document with specific people; share document using email, present document online, and share as a blog post
Export	export document as PDF or XPS document; change file type
Close	close currently open document
Account	user information, connected services, product information
Options	Word Options dialog box with options for customizing Word
Feedback	opens window with options for providing feedback to Microsoft on Microsoft products

Check Your Work Compare your work to the model answer to ensure that you have completed the activity correctly.

In Addition

Understanding Default Document Formatting

A Word document is based on a template that applies default formatting. Default formatting refers to formatting automatically applied by Word. Some of the default formats include 11-point Calibri as the font, line spacing of 1.08, and 8 points of spacing after each paragraph (added when you press the Enter key). You will learn more about fonts and paragraph spacing in Section 2.

Correcting Errors

Word contains a spelling feature that inserts wavy red lines below words it cannot find in the Spelling dictionary. You can edit these words or leave them as written. The wavy red lines do not print.

As you are working in a document that you previously saved and named, consider saving any new information you enter in the document. This way, if the power is disrupted or some other issue occurs with the software or hardware, you have the most recent version of your document saved. To save a document with the same name, click the Save button on the Quick Access Toolbar or click the File tab and then click the *Save* option at the backstage area. When you are finished working in Word, close any open documents and then close Word. Close a document by clicking the File tab and then clicking the *Close* option at the backstage area. Close Word by clicking the Close button in the upper right corner of the screen.

What You Will Do   Your supervisor has asked you to include additional information in the Moment's Notice Travel Package document you created.

Tutorial
Saving with the Same Name

Tutorial
Closing a Document and Closing Word

1   With **1-FCTTravelPkg.docx** open, make sure the insertion point is positioned at the end of the paragraph and then press the Enter key.

2   Type 3588 Ventura Boulevard.

3   Press Shift + Enter and then type Los Angeles, CA 90102.

Moment's Notice Travel Package

First Choice Travel
Los Angeles Office

Are you spontaneous and enjoy doi
will be interested in the First Choice
you can fly from New York to Londo
must make your reservation within

3588 Ventura Boulevard
Los Angeles, CA 90102

Step 2

Step 3

4   Save the document with the added text by clicking the Save button 🖫 on the Quick Access Toolbar.

Step 4

File   Home   Insert

Cut
Copy
Paste
Format Painter
Clipboard

Cal
B

5   Add additional text to the document by pressing Shift + Enter and then typing 213-555-7800.

Save Document with Same Name
Click Save button on Quick Access Toolbar.
OR
1. Click File tab.
2. Click *Save* option.

Close Document
1. Click File tab.
2. Click *Close* option.

Close Word
Click Close button.

6 Save the document with the added text by clicking the File tab and then clicking the *Save* option at the backstage area.

> If you are working in a document that has not been saved, clicking the Save button on the Quick Access Toolbar or clicking the File tab and then clicking the *Save* option will cause the Save As backstage area to display.

7 Close the document by clicking the File tab and then clicking the *Close* option at the backstage area.

8 Close Word by clicking the Close button in the upper right corner of the screen.

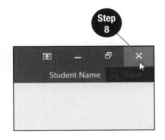

Check Your Work — Compare your work to the model answer to ensure that you have completed the activity correctly.

In Addition

Naming a Document

Document names created in Word and other applications in the Office suite can be up to 255 characters in length, including the drive letter, folder names, server name, and spaces. File names cannot include any of the characters in the table at the right.

Symbol Name	Symbol
forward slash	/
backslash	\
greater-than symbol	>
less-than symbol	<
asterisk	*
question mark	?
quotation mark	"
colon	:
pipe symbol	|

An existing document can be opened from the *Recent* option list at the Open backstage area, from a folder in OneDrive, or from the computer's hard drive or removable disk. In this activity, you will open a document from the WordS1 folder on your USB flash drive. (If you saved your student data files in a location or folder other than a USB flash drive, check with your instructor for specific steps.) After you create a document, you will often want to make changes to it. These changes may include adding text, called *inserting*, or removing text, called *deleting*. Before inserting or deleting text, position the insertion point at the desired location using the keyboard or the mouse. Use the Backspace key or Delete key on the keyboard to delete text.

What You Will Do First Choice Travel marketing staff members have reviewed your document on vacation specials and recommended a few changes. You need to create a revised version.

Tutorial

Opening a Document from a Removable Disk

Tutorial

Moving the Insertion Point and Inserting and Deleting Text

1 At the blank Word screen, click the File tab.

This displays the Open backstage area. If you have a document open and click the File tab, you will need to click the *Open* option to display the Open backstage area.

2 At the Open backstage area, click the *Browse* option.

3 In the Navigation pane of the Open dialog box, click the drive where your USB flash drive is located (such as *Removable Disk (F:)*).

Press Ctrl + F12 to display the Open dialog box without displaying the Open backstage area.

4 Double-click the *WordS1* folder in the Content pane.

5 Double-click *FCTVacSpecials.docx* in the Content pane.

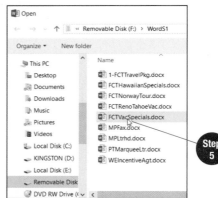

6 With the document open, click the File tab and then click the *Save As* option.

7 At the Save As backstage area, click the *Browse* option. (This should display the Save As dialog box with the WordS1 folder active on your storage medium.)

8 At the Save As dialog box, press the Home key to move the insertion point to the beginning of the file name in the *File name* text box, type 1-, and then press the Enter key. (The document name in the *File name* text box should display as **1-FCTVacSpecials.docx**.)

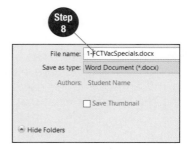

Pressing the Home key saves you from having to type the entire document name. To open the Save As dialog box without displaying the Save As backstage area, press F12.

9 Position the mouse pointer at the beginning of the second paragraph and then click the left mouse button.

This moves the insertion point to the location of the mouse pointer.

In Brief

Open Document from Removable Disk
1. Press Ctrl + F12.
2. In Navigation pane, click drive containing removable disk.
3. Double-click folder in Content pane.
4. Double-click document.

10 Press the Up, Down, Left, and Right arrow keys located to the right of the regular keys on the keyboard.

Use the information shown in Table 1.3 to practice moving the insertion point.

11 Press Ctrl + Home to move the insertion point to the beginning of the document.

12 Click at the beginning of the paragraph that begins *Sign up today for* and then type Ocean Vista Cruise Lines announces the inaugural voyage of the Pacific Sky ocean liner. Press the spacebar after typing the period.

By default, text you type is inserted in the document and existing text is moved to the right.

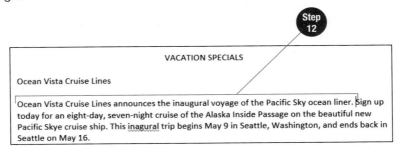

13 Press Ctrl + End to move the insertion point to the end of the document and then click anywhere in the last sentence in the document (the sentence that begins *Let First Choice Travel take*).

14 Press the Backspace key until the insertion point is positioned at the left margin and then press the Delete key until you have deleted the remainder of the sentence.

Pressing the Backspace key deletes any characters to the left of the insertion point. Press the Delete key to delete any characters to the right of the insertion point.

15 Click the Save button on the Quick Access Toolbar.

Clicking the Save button saves the document with the same name (**1-FCTVacSpecials.docx**).

Table 1.3 Insertion Point Keyboard Commands

Press	To move insertion point
End	to end of line
Home	to beginning of line
Page Up	up one screen
Page Down	down one screen
Ctrl + Home	to beginning of document
Ctrl + End	to end of document

Check Your Work Compare your work to the model answer to ensure that you have completed the activity correctly.

In Addition

Adding Buttons to the Quick Access Toolbar

You can add to the Quick Access Toolbar buttons that represent commonly used features. For example, you might want to add the Open button to save steps when opening a document or the Quick Print button to save steps when printing a document. To add a button to the Quick Access Toolbar, click the Customize Quick Access Toolbar button at the right side of the toolbar and then click the desired button name at the drop-down list.

In addition to moving the insertion point to a specific location, you can use the mouse to move the display of text in the document screen. Use the mouse with the vertical scroll bar to scroll through text in a document. The vertical scroll bar displays toward the right side of the screen. Scrolling in a document changes the text displayed but does not move the insertion point. Previously, you learned to delete text by pressing the Backspace key or the Delete key. You can also select text and then delete it, replace it with other text, or apply formatting to it. If you make a change to text, such as deleting it, and then change your mind, use the Undo and/or Redo buttons on the Quick Access Toolbar.

FIRST CHOICE TRAVEL

What You Will Do   The assistant manager, Jordan Keyes, has reviewed the document and asked you to make a few changes.

Tutorial
Scrolling

Tutorial
Selecting, Replacing, and Deleting Text

Tutorial
Using Undo and Redo

1. With **1-FCTVacSpecials.docx** open, press Ctrl + Home to move the insertion point to the beginning of the document.

2. Position the mouse pointer on the down scroll arrow on the vertical scroll bar and then click the left mouse button several times.

> This scrolls down the lines of text in the document. Scrolling changes the display of text but does not move the insertion point.

3. Position the mouse pointer on the vertical scroll bar below the scroll box and then click the left mouse button two times.

> The scroll box on the vertical scroll bar indicates the location of the text in the document screen in relation to the remainder of the document. Clicking below the scroll box on the vertical scroll bar scrolls down one screen of text at a time.

4. Position the mouse pointer on the scroll box on the vertical scroll bar, click and hold down the left mouse button, drag the scroll box to the top of the vertical scroll bar, and then release the mouse button.

5. Position the mouse pointer anywhere in the word *Behold* (located immediately after the first bullet) and then double-click the left mouse button to select it.

> Selected text displays with a gray background. You can also drag through text with the mouse to select it. When you select text, the Mini toolbar displays. You will learn more about the Mini toolbar in Activity 2.1.

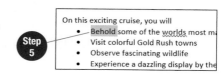

6. Type View.

> When you type *View*, it replaces *Behold*.

7. Move the insertion point to the beginning of the word *Glacier* (located in the second paragraph under the *Ocean Vista Cruise Lines* heading) and then press the F8 function key on the keyboard. Press the Right Arrow key until the words *Glacier Bay and* are selected.

> Pressing the F8 function key turns on Extend mode. Use the insertion point movement keys to select text in Extend mode.

8 Press the Delete key.

9 Hold down the Ctrl key, click anywhere in the first sentence of the second paragraph (begins with *Ocean Vista Cruise Lines announces*), and then release the Ctrl key.

> Holding down the Ctrl key while clicking the mouse button selects the entire sentence.

10 Press the Delete key to delete the selected sentence.

11 Click the Undo button ↶ ▾ on the Quick Access Toolbar.

> When you click the Undo button, the deleted sentence reappears. Clicking the Undo button reverses the last command or deletes the last entry you typed. Click the arrow at the right side of the Undo button and a drop-down list displays the changes made to the document since it was opened. Click an action to undo it and any actions listed above it in the drop-down list.

12 Click the Redo button ↷ on the Quick Access Toolbar.

> Clicking the Redo button deletes the selected sentence. If you click the Undo button and then decide you do not want to reverse the original action, click the Redo button.

13 Position the mouse pointer between the left edge of the page and the first line of text in the second paragraph until the pointer turns into an arrow pointing up and to the right (instead of the left) and then click the left mouse button.

> The space between the left edge of the page and the text is referred to as the **selection bar**. Use the selection bar to select specific amounts of text. Refer to Table 1.4 for more information on selecting text.

14 Deselect the text by clicking in the document.

> Deselecting cancels the selection of text.

15 Save the document by clicking the Save button on the Quick Access Toolbar.

Table 1.4 Selecting with the Mouse

To select	Complete these steps using the mouse
a word	Double-click the word.
a line of text	Click in the selection bar to the left of the line.
multiple lines of text	Drag in the selection bar to the left of the lines.
a sentence	Hold down the Ctrl key and then click anywhere in the sentence.
a paragraph	Double-click in the selection bar next to the paragraph or triple-click anywhere in the paragraph.
multiple paragraphs	Drag in the selection bar.
an entire document	Triple-click in the selection bar.

Check Your Work Compare your work to the model answer to ensure that you have completed the activity correctly.

In Addition

Resuming Reading or Editing a Document

When you work in a multiple-page document and then close the document, Word remembers where the insertion point was last positioned. When you reopen the document, Word displays a Welcome Back message at the right side of the screen near the vertical scroll bar.

The message tells you that you can pick up where you left off and identifies the page where your insertion point was last located. Click the message and the insertion point is positioned at the top of that page.

Activity 1.5 Checking Spelling and Grammar

Use Word's spelling checker to find and correct misspelled words and find duplicated words (such as *and and*). The spelling checker compares words in your document with words in its dictionary. If a match is found, the word is passed over. If no match is found for the word, the spelling checker stops, selects the word, and offers replacements. The grammar checker will search a document for grammar, punctuation, and word usage errors. The spelling checker and the grammar checker can help you create a well-written document but these features do not replace the need for proofreading.

What You Will Do   Continuing with the editing process, you are ready to check the spelling and grammar in the First Choice Travel vacation specials document.

Checking Spelling and Grammar

1 With **1-FCTVacSpecials.docx** open, press Ctrl + Home to move the insertion point to the beginning of the document.

2 Click the Review tab and then click the Spelling & Grammar button in the Proofing group.

> When you click the Spelling & Grammar button, Word selects the first misspelled word and displays the Spelling task pane at the right side of the screen with options for correcting the error, ignoring the error, or adding the word to the spelling dictionary. It also contains a brief definition of the selected word in the list box. If a grammar error is selected, the Grammar task pane displays.

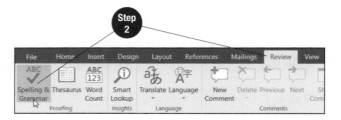

3 When the word *inagural* is selected in the document and *inaugural* is selected in the list box in the Spelling task pane, click the Change button in the pane.

> Refer to Table 1.5 for an explanation of the buttons in the Spelling task pane and Grammar task pane.

4 When the word *worlds* is selected in the document and *world's* is selected in the list box in the Grammar task pane, click the Change button.

5 When the word *Your* is selected in the document and *You* is selected in the list box in the Grammar task pane, click the Change button.

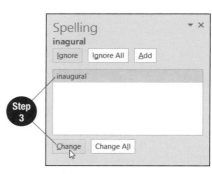

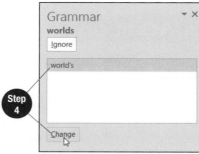

In Brief

Check Spelling and Grammar
1. Click Review tab.
2. Click Spelling & Grammar button.
3. Ignore or change as needed.
4. Click OK.

6 When the word *the* is selected (this word occurs twice), click the Delete button in the Spelling task pane.

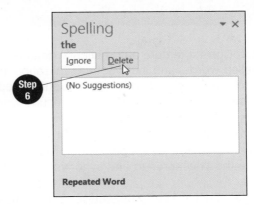

Step 6

7 When the word *of* is selected in the document and *off* is selected in the list box in the Grammar task pane, click the Change button.

8 When the word *utah* is selected in the document and *Utah* is selected in the list box in the Spelling task pane, click the Change button.

9 Click OK at the message box telling you the spelling and grammar check is complete.

10 Click the Save button on the Quick Access Toolbar to save the changes made to the document.

Table 1.5 Spelling Task Pane and Grammar Task Pane Buttons

Button	Function
Ignore	during spell checking, skips that occurrence of the word; in grammar checking, leaves currently selected text as written
Ignore All	during spell checking, skips that occurrence and all other occurrences of the word in the document
Add	adds selected word to the main spelling check dictionary
Delete	deletes the currently selected word(s)
Change	replaces selected word in sentence with selected word in list box
Change All	replaces selected word in sentence with selected word in list box and all other occurrences of the word

Check Your Work ▶ Compare your work to the model answer to ensure that you have completed the activity correctly.

In Addition

Changing Spelling Options

Control spelling and grammar checking options at the Word Options dialog box with the *Proofing* option selected. Display this dialog box by clicking the File tab and then clicking *Options*. At the Word Options dialog box, click *Proofing* in the left panel of the dialog box. With options in the dialog box, you can tell the spelling checker to ignore certain types of text, create custom dictionaries, show readability statistics, and hide spelling and/or grammar errors in the document.

Editing While Checking Spelling and Grammar

When checking a document, you can temporarily leave the Spelling task pane or Grammar task pane by clicking in the document. To resume the spelling and grammar check, click the Resume button in the Spelling task pane or Grammar task pane.

The AutoCorrect feature automatically detects and corrects some typographical errors, misspelled words, and incorrect capitalization. In addition to correcting errors, you can use the AutoCorrect feature to insert frequently used text. Use the Thesaurus to find synonyms, antonyms, and related terms for a particular word.

What You Will Do You need to insert additional text in the First Choice Travel vacation specials document. To speed up the process, you will add an entry to AutoCorrect. You will also use the Thesaurus to find synonyms for specific words in the document.

Tutorial
Adding and Deleting
an AutoCorrect Entry

Tutorial
Using the Thesaurus

1. With **1-FCTVacSpecials.docx** open, click the File tab and then click *Options*.

2. At the Word Options dialog box, click *Proofing* in the left panel and then click the AutoCorrect Options button in the *AutoCorrect options* section.

3. At the AutoCorrect dialog box, type bst in the *Replace* text box and then press the Tab key.

4. Type Bahamas Sightseeing Tour in the *With* text box and then click the Add button.

5. Click OK to close the AutoCorrect dialog box.

6. Click OK to close the Word Options dialog box.

7. Press Ctrl + End to move the insertion point to the end of the document, make sure the insertion point is positioned a double space below the last bulleted item, and then type the text shown in Figure 1.3. (Type the text exactly as shown. AutoCorrect will correct *bst* to *Bahamas Sightseeing Tour* when you press the Enter key or the spacebar.)

Figure 1.3 Step 7

bst

The Bahamas consist of over 700 islands and cays, all with friendly people, beautiful beaches, and magnificent dive spots. First Choice Travel offers the bst to explore these exciting and breathtaking islands. Sign up for the bst and experience the bustling city of Nassau, which offers everything from parasailing to casino gaming. Call us to discover how you can join the bst at an incredibly low price.

8 Click anywhere in the word *breathtaking* (located in the second sentence in the paragraph you just typed), click the Review tab, and then click the Thesaurus button 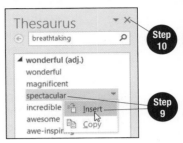 in the Proofing group.

9 At the Thesaurus task pane, right-click the word *spectacular* in the task pane list box and then click *Insert* at the drop-down list.

> You can also hover the mouse pointer over the desired word in the task pane list box, click the arrow that displays at the right side of the word, and then click *Insert* at the drop-down list.

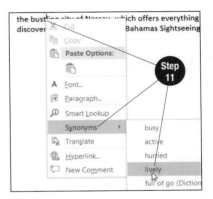

10 Close the Thesaurus task pane by clicking the Close button ✕ in the upper right corner of the task pane.

11 Position the mouse pointer on the word *bustling* (located in the third sentence in the paragraph you just typed) and then click the right mouse button. At the shortcut menu that displays, point to *Synonyms* and then click *lively* at the side menu.

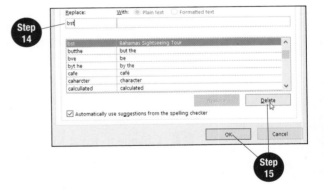

12 Click the Save button to save the document with the same name.

13 Click the File tab and then click *Options*. At the Word Options dialog box, click *Proofing* in the left panel and then click the AutoCorrect Options button.

14 At the AutoCorrect dialog box, type bst in the *Replace* text box.

> This selects *bst* and *Bahamas Sightseeing Tour* in the list box.

15 Click the Delete button and then click OK to close the dialog box.

16 Click OK to close the Word Options dialog box.

Check Your Work Compare your work to the model answer to ensure that you have completed the activity correctly.

In Addition

Using the Thesaurus Task Pane

Depending on the word you are looking up, the words in the Thesaurus task pane list box may display followed by *(n.)* for *noun*, *(v.)* for *verb*, *(adj.)* for *adjective*, or *(adv.)* for *adverb*. Click a word in the list box and a definition of the word displays below the list box. (You may need to install a dictionary before you will see a definition. To install a dictionary, click the <u>Get a Dictionary</u> hyperlink. At the Dictionaries pane, click the desired dictionary and then click the Download button.)

Changing Document Views; Hiding and Showing White Space

By default, a document displays in Print Layout view. This view displays the document on the screen as it will appear when printed. Other views are available, such as Read Mode, Web Layout, Outline, or Draft. Change views with buttons in the view area on the Status bar or with options in the Views group on the View tab. Change to Draft view and the document displays in a format for efficient editing and formatting. The Read Mode displays a document in a format for easy viewing and reading. Change to Web Layout view to display a document as it would appear as a web page. In Print Layout view, a page displays as it will appear when printed, including the white space at the top and bottom of the page representing the document's margins. To save space on the screen, the white space can be removed using the Hide White Space icon. Redisplay white space using the Show White Space icon.

What You Will Do   Several people will be reviewing the First Choice Travel vacation specials document on-screen, so you decide to experiment with various views to determine the best one for on-screen reviewing.

Tutorial
Changing Document Views

Tutorial
Hiding and Showing White Space

1 With **1-FCTVacSpecials.docx** open, press Ctrl + Home to move the insertion point to the beginning of the document.

2 Change to Draft view by clicking the View tab and then clicking the Draft button in the Views group.

Change to Draft view to display the document in a format designed for efficient editing and formatting. In Draft view, margins and other features such as headers and footers do not display.

3 Change to Web Layout view by clicking the Web Layout button in the view area on the Status bar (see Figure 1.4).

Change to Web Layout view to display the document as it would appear as a web page.

4 Change to Read Mode by clicking the Read Mode button in the Views group.

Read Mode displays a document for easy viewing and reading. You can also display a document in Read Mode by clicking the Read Mode button in the view area of the Status bar.

5 Display the next two pages on the screen by clicking the Next button (right-pointing triangle in a circle) that displays at the right side of the screen.

Figure 1.4 View Buttons in View Area on Status Bar

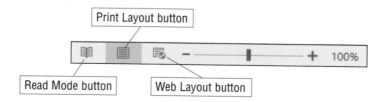

In Brief

Display Draft View
1. Click View tab.
2. Click Draft button.

Display Read Mode View
1. Click View tab.
2. Click Read Mode button.
OR
Click Read Mode button on Status bar.

Display Web Layout View
1. Click View tab.
2. Click Web Layout button.
OR
Click Web Layout button on Status bar.

6 Display previous pages by clicking the Previous button (left-pointing triangle in a circle) that displays at the left side of the screen.

7 Continue navigating in Read Mode using the keyboard commands shown in Table 1.6.

8 Return to Print Layout view by pressing the Esc key.

Pressing the Esc key displays the document in Print Layout view. You can also return to Print Layout view by clicking the View tab and then clicking *Edit Document* at the drop-down list.

9 To save space on the screen, remove the white space that displays at the top and bottom of each page as well as the gray space between pages. To do this, position the mouse pointer on the gray space above the page until the pointer turns into the hide white space icon ⊞ and then double-click the left mouse button.

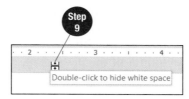

10 Scroll through the document and then redisplay the white and gray space at the top and bottom of each page. To do this, position the mouse pointer on the gray line at the top of the page until the pointer turns into a show white space icon ⊞ and then double-click the left mouse button.

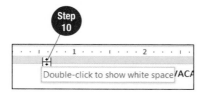

Table 1.6 Navigating in Read Mode

Press this key	To complete this action
Page Down or spacebar	Move to next page or section.
Page Up or Backspace key	Move to previous page or section.
Right Arrow	Move to next page.
Left Arrow	Move to previous page.
Home	Move to first page in document.
End	Move to last page in document.
Esc	Return to previous view.

In Addition

Zooming In on an Object in Read Mode

If your document contains an object such as an image, shape, SmartArt, or table, you can zoom in on the object in Read Mode by double-clicking the object. The object appears larger on the screen and a button containing a diagonally pointing arrow displays just outside the upper right corner of it. Click this button to zoom in even more on the object. Click once outside the object to return it to its original size.

By default, a document displays at 100%. This display percentage can be changed with the Zoom slider bar located at the right side of the Status bar and with options in the Zoom group on the View tab. To change display percentage with the Zoom slider bar, drag the button on the bar to increase or decrease the percentage, or click the Zoom Out button to decrease the display percentage or the Zoom In button to increase the percentage. Use buttons in the Zoom group on the View tab to return to the 100% display percentage, display one page or multiple pages, expand the document across the screen, and display the Zoom dialog box.

What You Will Do   Several people will be reviewing the First Choice Travel vacation specials document on the screen so you decide to experiment with various views and zoom percentages to determine the best view for on-screen reviewing.

Tutorial

Changing the Display Percentage

1. With **1-FCTVacSpecials.docx** open, press Ctrl + Home to move the insertion point to the beginning of the document.

2. Click the Zoom Out button ⊟ at the left side of the Zoom slider bar to decrease the display percentage to 90%.

    Figure 1.5 identifies the Zoom slider bar along with Zoom Out and Zoom In buttons.

3. Click the Zoom In button ⊞ at the right side of the Zoom slider bar to increase the display percentage to 100%.

4. Position the mouse pointer on the Zoom slider button on the Zoom slider bar, click and hold down the left mouse button, drag to the right to increase the display percentage, drag left to decrease the percentage, and then release the mouse button.

5. Click the View tab.

6. Click the 100% button in the Zoom group to return to the default display percentage of 100%.

7. Click the One Page button in the Zoom group to display just the first page on the screen.

8. Click the Multiple Pages button in the Zoom group to display all of the pages on the screen.

9. Click the Zoom button in the Zoom group to display the Zoom dialog box.

    You can also display the Zoom dialog box by clicking the Zoom level button (the percentage that displays at the right side of the Zoom slider bar).

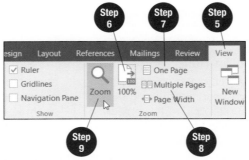

10 Click the *75%* option in the *Zoom to* section of the dialog box.

11 Click OK to close the Zoom dialog box.

The document displays at 75%.

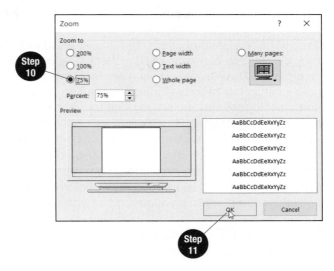

12 Click the 100% button in the Zoom group to return to the default display percentage.

Figure 1.5 Zoom Slider Bar

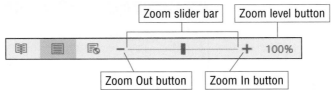

In Addition

Working with Windows

The Window group on the View tab contains a number of buttons for working with windows. Click the New Window button to open a new window containing the same document. This is useful if you want to view a portion of the document while editing in another location. If more than one document is open, the documents can be arranged so that a portion of each is visible. To do this, click the Arrange All button in the Window group. Click the Split button in the Window group to split the open document in two with a split bar and another horizontal ruler. Splitting a window is useful if you want to view different parts of a document at one time. Compare the contents of two documents by opening both documents and then clicking the View Side by Side button in the Window group. Both documents display on the screen arranged side by side. By default, synchronous scrolling is active, which means that scrolling in one document results in the same scrolling in the other document. Turn off synchronous scrolling by clicking the Synchronous Scrolling button.

Use the Navigation pane to browse in a document or search for specific text or items. Display the Navigation pane by clicking the Find button in the Editing group on the Home tab or by clicking the *Navigation Pane* check box in the Show group on the View tab to insert a check mark. The Navigation pane contains three tabs—Headings, Pages, and Results. Click the Headings tab to display in the Navigation pane thumbnails of each page. Click a page thumbnail to move the insertion point to that page. Search for text by clicking in the search text box and then typing the desired text. With the Pages tab active, each occurrence of the search text is highlighted in the pages. Click the Results tab to display each occurrence of the search text along with the text that displays before and after each occurrence.

What You Will Do   Review the First Choice Travel vacation specials document by using the Navigation pane to navigate and search for specific text in the document.

Tutorial
Navigating Using the Navigation Pane

Tutorial
Finding Text

1 With **1-FCTVacSpecials.docx** open, display the Navigation pane by clicking the View tab and then clicking the *Navigation Pane* check box to insert a check mark.

> You can also display the Navigation pane by clicking the Find button in the Editing group on the Home tab.

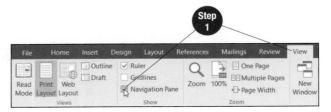

2 Click the Pages tab in the Navigation pane.

> Clicking the Pages tab displays thumbnails of each page in the Navigation pane.

3 Click the page 2 thumbnail in the Navigation pane.

> Clicking the page 2 thumbnail moves the insertion point to the beginning of page 2.

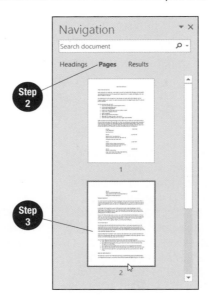

In Brief

Display Navigation Pane
1. Click View tab.
2. Click *Navigation Pane* check box.
OR
1. Click Home tab.
2. Click Find button.

4 Click the page 1 thumbnail in the Navigation pane.

5 Click in the search text box in the Navigation pane (contains the text *Search document*) and then type Pacific Skye.

After you type *Pacific Skye*, each occurrence of the text is highlighted in the document.

6 Click the Next Search Result button in the Navigation pane (displays as a down arrow) to select the next occurrence of *Pacific Skye*. Click the button again to select the next occurrence.

You can click the Previous Search Result button (displays as an up arrow) to display the previous occurrence of the search text.

7 Click the Results tab to display in the Navigation pane each occurrence of the search text *Pacific Skye* along with the text that displays before and after each occurrence.

8 Select the first occurrence of *Pacific Skye* in the document by clicking the first item in the Navigation pane.

9 Click the X at the right side of the search text box.

Clicking this button ends the current search, removes the search text in the Navigation pane, and selects the current search result in the document.

10 Close the Navigation pane by clicking the Close button in the upper right corner of the pane.

You can also close the Navigation pane by clicking the *Navigation Pane* check box in the Show group on the View tab to remove the check mark.

In Addition

Displaying Ribbon Options

Control how much of the ribbon displays on screen with the Ribbon Display Options button in the upper right corner of the screen. Click this button and a drop-down list displays with options for hiding the ribbon, showing only the tabs, or showing tabs and commands. You can also turn off the display of the ribbon by clicking the Collapse the Ribbon button located above the vertical scroll bar or with the keyboard shortcut Ctrl + F1. Redisplay the ribbon by double-clicking any tab or by pressing Ctrl + F1.

Activity 1.10 Finding and Replacing Text

In the previous activity you used the Navigation pane to find all occurrences of specific text in the document. If you want to find text and then replace it with other text, use options at the Find and Replace dialog box with the Replace tab selected. Display this dialog box by clicking the Replace button in the Editing group on the Home tab.

What You Will Do   As you review the vacation specials document, you discover that the name of the ship is spelled incorrectly and that the ship's cabins are divided into categories rather than classes. You decide to use the Find and Replace feature to correct these errors.

Tutorial
Finding and Replacing Text

1 With **1-FCTVacSpecials.docx** open, press Ctrl + Home to move the insertion point to the beginning of the document.

2 The name of the ship is the *Pacific Sky*, not the *Pacific Skye*. To change the name, display the Find and Replace dialog box by clicking the Home tab and then clicking the Replace button in the Editing group.

3 At the Find and Replace dialog box with the Replace tab selected, type Skye in the *Find what* text box and then press the Tab key.

Pressing the Tab key moves the insertion point to the *Replace with* text box. You can also click in the *Replace with* text box.

4 Type Sky in the *Replace with* text box.

5 Click the Replace All button at the bottom of the dialog box.

Clicking the Replace All button replaces all occurrences of the text in the document. If you want control over what is replaced in a document, click the Replace button to replace text or click the Find Next button to move to the next occurrence of the text.

6 At the message telling you that four replacements were made, click OK.

7 Click the Close button to close the Find and Replace dialog box.

8 The word *class* is used to designate cabins, when it should instead be *category*. To make this change, click the Replace button in the Editing group on the Home tab.

9 At the Find and Replace dialog box with the Replace tab selected, type class.

When you open the Replace dialog box, *Skye* is automatically selected in the *Find what* text box. When you begin typing *class*, the selected text is automatically deleted.

10 Press the Tab key and then type category in the *Replace with* text box.

When you type the find text and the replace text in all lowercase letters, Word will find and replace all occurrences regardless of the capitalization. For example, Word will find *Class* in the document and replace it with *Category*.

11 Click the Replace All button.

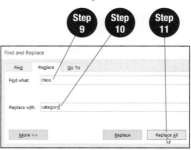

In Brief

Find and Replace Text
1. Click Replace button.
2. Type find text.
3. Press Tab key.
4. Type replace text.
5. Click Replace or Replace All button.
6. Click OK.
7. Click Close button.

12 At the message telling you that six replacements were made, click OK.

13 Click the Close button to close the Find and Replace dialog box.

14 Click the Save button on the Quick Access Toolbar to save the document.

Check Your Work Compare your work to the model answer to ensure that you have completed the activity correctly.

In Addition

Exploring Options at the Expanded Find and Replace Dialog Box

The Find and Replace dialog box contains a variety of check boxes with options you can choose for completing a find and replace. To display these options, click the More button located at the bottom of the dialog box. This causes the Find and Replace dialog box to expand as shown at the right. The options are described in the table below.

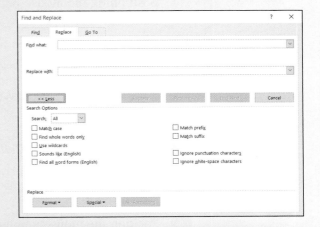

Option	Action
Match case	Exactly match the case of the search text. For example, if you search for *Book*, Word will stop at *Book* but not *book* or *BOOK*.
Find whole words only	Find a whole word, not a part of a word. For example, if you search for *her* and did not select *Find whole words only*, Word would stop at t*her*e, *her*e, *her*s, and so on.
Use wildcards	Search for wildcards, special characters, or special search operators.
Sounds like	Match words that sound alike but are spelled differently, such as *know* and *no*.
Find all word forms	Find all forms of the word entered in the *Find what* text box. For example, if you enter *hold*, Word will stop at *held* and *holding*.
Match prefix	Find only those words that begin with the letters in the *Find what* text box. For example, if you enter *per*, Word will stop at words such as *perform* and *perfect* but will skip over words such as *super* and *hyperlink*.
Match suffix	Find only those words that end with the letters in the *Find what* text box. For example, if you enter *ly*, Word will stop at words such as *accurately* and *quietly* but skip over words such as *catalyst* and *lyre*.
Ignore punctuation characters	Ignore punctuation within characters. For example, if you enter *US* in the *Find what* text box, Word will stop at *U.S.*
Ignore white-space characters	Ignore spaces between letters. For example, if you enter *F B I* in the *Find what* text box, Word will stop at *FBI*.

Word includes the Tell Me feature, which provides information and guidance on how to complete a function. To use Tell Me, click in the *Tell Me* text box on the ribbon to the right of the View tab and then type the function for which you want help. As you type, a drop-down list displays with options that are refined as you continue typing, a feature referred to as *word-wheeling*. The drop-down list displays options for completing the function, displaying information on the function from sources on the web, or displaying information on the function in the Word Help window. When you first click in the *Tell Me* text box, the drop-down list will contain the last five functions you entered.

What You Will Do   To enhance the appearance of the document, you decide to use the Tell Me feature to change the font color of the title *VACATION SPECIALS*. You will also use the Tell Me feature to access the Word Help window and find articles on AutoCorrect.

Tutorial
Using the Tell Me Feature

1 With **1-FCTVacSpecials.docx** open, select the title *VACATION SPECIALS* by positioning the mouse pointer in the title and then triple-clicking the left mouse button.

2 Click in the *Tell Me* text box.

> The *Tell Me* text box is located on the ribbon to the right of the View tab and contains the text *Tell me what you want to do*. When you click in the text box, the last five functions entered will display in a drop-down list.

3 Type font color in the *Tell Me* text box.

> A drop-down list displays with options such as *Font Color*, *Font Size*, *Border Color*, *Text Highlight Color*, and *Font*.

4 Position the mouse pointer on the *Font Color* option in the drop-down list.

5 At the side menu that displays, click the *Blue* color option in the *Standard Colors* section.

> The Blue font color is applied to the selected title. The Tell Me feature guided you through the process of applying font color without you having to learn how to apply font color using a button on the ribbon or an option at a dialog box.

6 The Tell Me feature also includes access to the Word Help window. To display the Word Help window with information on AutoCorrect, click in the *Tell Me* text box and then type AutoCorrect.

7 At the drop-down list, click *Get Help on "AutoCorrect"*.

> The Word Help window opens with articles on AutoCorrect.

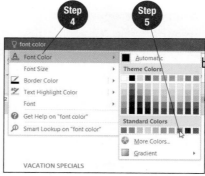

8 At the Word Help window, click the first hyperlink in the window list box.

Clicking the hyperlink opens the article in the Word Help window.

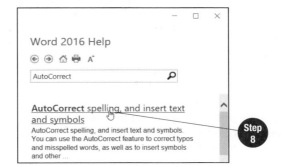

9 The Word Help window contains five buttons for navigating and managing the window. Click the Back button (contains a left-pointing arrow) in the Word Help window to display the previous window.

10 Click the Forward button (contains a right-pointing arrow) to redisplay the article on AutoCorrect.

11 Click the Use Large Text button to increase the size of text in the window.

Print information on a topic or feature by clicking the Print button and then clicking the Print button at the Print dialog box.

12 Click the Home button to return to the home screen of the Word Help window.

13 Close the Word Help window by clicking the Close button in the upper right corner of the window.

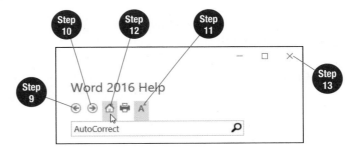

Check Your Work   Compare your work to the model answer to ensure that you have completed the activity correctly.

In Addition

Accessing Smart Lookup

Using the Smart Lookup feature, you can access information on a function from a variety of sources on the web such as Wikipedia, Bing, and the Oxford dictionary. The Tell Me feature is one way to access Smart Lookup. To use Tell Me for Smart Lookup, click in the *Tell Me* text box, type the function on which you want to display information, and then click the *Smart Lookup* option in the drop-down list. Clicking the *Smart Lookup* option displays the Smart Lookup task pane at the right side of the screen with information on the function from a variety of locations on the Internet. Smart Lookup can also be accessed with the Smart Lookup button in the Insights group on the Review tab or by selecting text about which you want additional information, right-clicking the selected text, and then clicking *Smart Lookup* at the shortcut menu.

Activity 1.12 — Using the Help Feature; Previewing and Printing

The Word Help window can be opened through the Tell Me feature or by pressing the F1 function key on the keyboard. You can also open the Word Help window directly from dialog boxes or the backstage area. Display a dialog box and then click the Help button in the upper right corner and the Word Help window displays with specific information related to the dialog box. Display the backstage area and then click the Help button in the upper right corner of the screen and the Word Help window displays with information related to the specific backstage area. The Print backstage area provides options for previewing the document before printing, indicating the number of copies, specifying the pages for printing, and customizing the document.

What You Will Do   You are ready to print the First Choice Travel vacation specials document, but first you want to learn more about printing a document. You decide to experiment with the Help feature in a dialog box and backstage area and then use Help to learn about printing.

Tutorial
Using the Help Feature

Tutorial
Previewing
and Printing

1 With **1-FCTVacSpecials.docx** open, press Ctrl + Home to move the insertion point to the beginning of the document.

2 Click the Font group dialog box launcher  to display the Font dialog box.

> The Font group dialog box launcher is located in the lower right corner of the Font group and displays as a small button containing a diagonal arrow.

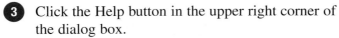
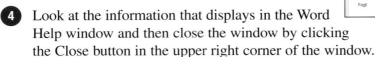

3 Click the Help button in the upper right corner of the dialog box.

4 Look at the information that displays in the Word Help window and then close the window by clicking the Close button in the upper right corner of the window.

5 Close the Font dialog box by clicking the Close button in the upper right corner of the dialog box.

6 Click the File tab to display the backstage area.

7 Click the Help button in the upper right corner of the backstage area.

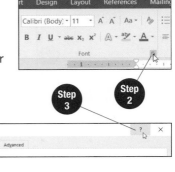

8 Look at the information that displays in the Word Help window and then close the window by clicking the Close button.

9 Click the Back button in the backstage area to return to the document.

10 Press the F1 function key to display the Word Help window.

11 Click in the Word Help window search text box, type print, and then press the Enter key.

12 Click a hyperlink in the Word Help window list box that pertains to printing a document.

13 Read the information and then close the window by clicking the Close button.

14 Click the File tab and then click the *Print* option to display the Print backstage area.

> At the Print backstage area, your document displays at the right side of the screen as it will appear when printed. The left side of the Print backstage area displays three

Print a Document
1. Click File tab.
2. Click *Print* option.
3. Click Print button.

Print a Specific Page
1. Click File tab.
2. Click *Print* option.
3. Click in *Pages* text box.
4. Type page number.
5. Click Print button.

Print Current Page
1. Position insertion point in page.
2. Click File tab.
3. Click *Print* option.
4. Click top gallery in *Settings* category.
5. Click *Print Current Page* at drop-down list.
6. Click Print button.

categories—*Print*, *Printer*, and *Settings*. Click the Print button in the *Print* category to send the document to the printer. Specify the number of copies you want printed with the *Copies* measurement box in the *Print* category. Use the gallery in the *Printer* category to specify the desired printer. The *Settings* category contains a number of galleries, each with options for specifying how you want your document printed.

15 Click twice on the Zoom In button at the right side of the Zoom slider bar.

Click the Zoom In button to increase the size of the page or click the Zoom Out button to decrease the size of the page.

16 Click the Next Page button located below and to the left of the preview page to display the next page in the document.

17 Click the Zoom to Page button located at the right side of the Zoom slider bar.

18 Print only page 2 of the document by clicking in the *Pages* text box (in the *Settings* category), typing 2, and then clicking the Print button.

19 Move the insertion point to any character in page 3 and then print page 3. Begin by clicking the File tab and then clicking the *Print* option.

20 At the Print backstage area, click the top gallery in the *Settings* category and then click *Print Current Page* at the drop-down list.

21 Click the Print button.

22 Save and then close **1-FCTVacSpecials.docx**.

Check Your Work Compare your work to the model answer to ensure that you have completed the activity correctly.

In Addition

Specifying Pages to Print

Identify a specific page, multiple pages, and/or a range of pages for printing at the Print backstage area. Print specific pages by clicking in the *Pages* text box and then typing the page numbers of the pages you want printed. To print specific multiple pages, use a comma to indicate *and* and use a hyphen to indicate *through*. For example, to print pages 2 and 5, type **2,5** in the *Pages* text box. To print pages 6 through 10, type **6-10**. You can enter both commas and hyphens when specifying page numbers.

Getting Help on a Button

When you hover the mouse pointer over certain buttons, the ScreenTip that displays includes a Help icon and the text *Tell me more*. Click this hyperlinked text and the Word Help window opens with information about the button feature. You can also hover the mouse pointer over a button and then press F1 to display the Word Help window with information about the button feature.

Word includes a number of template documents formatted for specific uses. Each Word document is based on a template document, with the Normal template as the default. With Word templates (and Microsoft online templates), you can easily create a variety of documents, such as letters, reports, and awards, with specialized formatting. Display available templates by clicking the File tab and then clicking the *New* option. At the New backstage area, click in the search text box, type a category, and then press the Enter key. Word displays templates matching the category. Click the desired template and then click the Create button. You must be connected to the Internet to download online templates.

What You Will Do　You are the projects coordinator for Marquee Productions, a movie production company. The company's travel agency is First Choice Travel, and you need the agency to make flight and hotel reservations for personnel involved in filming a movie in and around Toronto. You decide to use a letter template to help you format the letter.

Tutorial

Creating a Document Using a Template

1　Click the File tab and then click the *New* option.

2　At the New backstage area, click in the search text box (contains the text *Search for online templates*), type business letter equity theme, and then press the Enter key.

3　Click the first *Letter (Equity theme)* template in the backstage area.

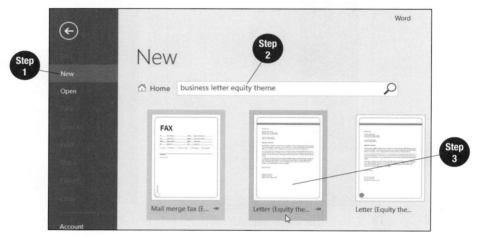

4　Click the Create button.

5　At the letter document, click the *[Pick the date]* placeholder and then type the current date. (Your date will automatically change to numbers when you click outside the placeholder.)

6　If necessary, select the name that displays below the date and then type your first and last names.

7　Click the *[Type the sender company name]* placeholder and then type Marquee Productions.

8　Click the *[Type the sender company address]* placeholder, type 955 South Alameda Street, press the Enter key, and then type Los Angeles, CA 90037.

9　Click the *[Type the recipient name]* placeholder and then type Ms. Melissa Gehring.

10　Press the Enter key and then type First Choice Travel.

In Brief

**Create Document
Using Template**
1. Click File tab.
2. Click *New* option.
3. Click template.
4. Click Create button.

11 Click the *[Type the recipient address]* placeholder, type 3588 Ventura Boulevard, press the Enter key, and then type Los Angeles, CA 90102.

12 Click the *[Type the salutation]* placeholder and then type Dear Ms. Gehring:.

13 Click anywhere in the three paragraphs of text in the body of the letter and then type the text shown in Figure 1.6.

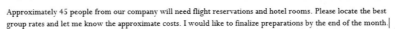

> **Dear Ms. Gehring:**
>
> Marquee Productions will be filming a movie in and around the Toronto area from July 9 through August 31, 2018. I would like scheduling and pricing information for flights from Los Angeles to Toronto, as well as information on lodging.
>
> Approximately 45 people from our company will need flight reservations and hotel rooms. Please locate the best group rates and let me know the approximate costs. I would like to finalize preparations by the end of the month.

Step 13

14 Click the *[Type the closing]* placeholder and then type Sincerely,.

15 Make sure your first and last names display below *Sincerely*. If not, select the current name below *Sincerely* and then type your first and last names.

16 Click the *[Type the sender title]* placeholder and then type Projects Coordinator.

17 Click the Save button on the Quick Access Toolbar.

18 At the Save As backstage area, navigate to the *WordS1* folder on your storage medium.

19 At the Save As dialog box with the WordS1 folder active, type 1-MPLtrtoFCT in the *File name* text box and then press the Enter key (or click the Save button).

20 Print the letter by clicking the File tab, clicking the *Print* option, and then clicking the Print button.

21 Close the document by clicking the File tab and then clicking the *Close* option.

Figure 1.6 Step 13

> Marquee Productions will be filming a movie in and around the Toronto area from July 9 through August 31, 2018. I would like scheduling and pricing information for flights from Los Angeles to Toronto, as well as information on lodging.
>
> Approximately 45 people from our company will need flight reservations and hotel rooms. Please locate the best group rates and let me know the approximate costs. I would like to finalize preparations by the end of the month.

Check Your Work Compare your work to the model answer to ensure that you have completed the activity correctly.

In Addition

Specifying a Template Category

When you search for online templates at the New backstage area, a *Category* list box displays at the right side of the screen. The list box displays the category and the number of templates that fit within the category. Click the desired category in the list box, and only templates matching that category will display in the New backstage area.

As you continue working with documents, consider document management tasks such as creating a folder and copying, moving, and deleting documents. You can complete many document management tasks related to one or more documents at the Open dialog box or Save As dialog box. By default, Word saves a file as a Word document and adds the extension *.docx* to the name. With the *Save as type* option at the Save As dialog box, you can save a document in a different format such as rich text or an earlier version of Word, or as a web page or plain text file.

What You Will Do   Since First Choice Travel will be communicating with Marquee Productions, you decide to create a folder into which you will insert Marquee Productions documents. You will also save a document in an older version of Word.

Tutorial
Managing Folders

Tutorial
Managing Documents

Tutorial
Saving in a Different Format

1 Click the File tab.

2 At the Open backstage area, click the *Browse* option.

3 At the Open dialog box, navigate to the WordS1 folder on your storage medium.

4 Click the New folder button.

5 Type Marquee and then press the Enter key.

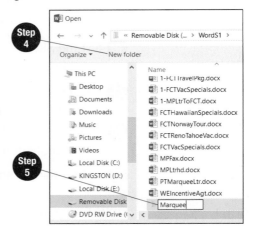

6 Click the document *MPFax.docx* in the Open dialog box Content pane, hold down the Ctrl key, click *1-FCTVacSpecials.docx*, and then release the Ctrl key.

> Use the Ctrl key to select nonadjacent documents. Use the Shift key to select adjacent documents.

7 Right-click either of the selected documents and then click *Copy* at the shortcut menu.

8 Double-click the *Marquee* folder.

> Folders display in the Open dialog box Content pane before documents. Folders display preceded by a file folder icon 📁 and documents display preceded by a document icon 📄.

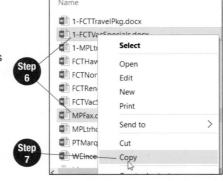

9 Position the mouse pointer in a white portion of the Open dialog box Content pane, click the right mouse button, and then click *Paste* at the shortcut menu.

> The copied documents are inserted in the Marquee folder.

10 You need to send **1-FCTVacSpecials.docx** to a colleague who uses Word 2003, so you need to save the document in that format. At the Open dialog box with the Marquee folder active, double-click *1-FCTVacSpecials.docx*.

11 Click the File tab and then click the *Save As* option.

12 At the Save As backstage area, click the *Browse* option.

13 At the Save As dialog box, make sure WordS1 is the active folder and then type 1-FCTVacSpecialsWd2003 in the *File name* text box.

14 Click the *Save as type* option box and then click *Word 97-2003 Document (*.doc)* at the drop-down list.

15 Click the Save button in the lower right corner of the dialog box.

> If a compatibility checker message displays, click the Continue button.

16 Close the document.

17 Press Ctrl + F12 to display the Open dialog box. If the WordS1 folder on your storage medium is not already the active folder, navigate to the WordS1 folder.

18 At the Open dialog box, rename the Marquee folder by right-clicking the folder name and then clicking *Rename* at the shortcut menu.

19 Type MarqueeProductions and then press the Enter key.

> The new folder name replaces the original folder name. You can also rename a folder by clicking the Organize button, clicking *Rename* at the drop-down list, and then typing the new folder name.

20 Delete the MarqueeProductions folder by first clicking the folder to select it.

21 Click the Organize button and then click *Delete* at the drop-down list.

22 At the message asking if you are sure you want to delete the folder and all of its contents, click the Yes button.

23 Close the Open dialog box.

24 Close Word by clicking the Close button in the upper right corner of the screen.

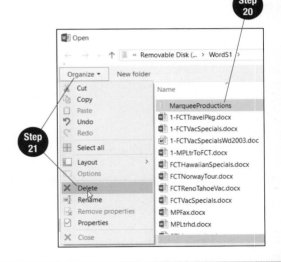

Check Your Work — Compare your work to the model answer to ensure that you have completed the activity correctly.

In Addition

Editing a PDF File in Word

PDF stands for Portable Document Format and is a common format for sharing files. A PDF file can be opened and edited in Word. When you open a PDF file, Word converts the file to a .docx file and the data in the file may not display in the exact format as in the PDF file. Converting a PDF file to a Word document works best with text-based documents.

Features Summary

Feature	Ribbon Tab, Group	Button	Quick Access Toolbar	File Tab Option	Keyboard Shortcut
AutoCorrect dialog box				*Options, Proofing, AutoCorrect Options*	
close document				*Close*	Ctrl + F4
close Word		✕			Alt + F4
collapse or redisplay ribbon					Ctrl + F1
Draft view	View, Views				
Extend mode					F8
Help					F1
hide white space					
Move insertion point to end of document					Ctrl + End
Move insertion point to start of document					Ctrl + Home
Navigation pane	View, Show				Ctrl + F
New backstage area				*New*	
New Line command					Shift + Enter
Open backstage area				*Open*	Ctrl + O
Open dialog box					Ctrl + F12
Print backstage area				*Print*	Ctrl + P
Print Layout view	View, Views				
Read Mode	View, Views				
redo (repeat) an action					Ctrl + Y
replace text	Home, Editing				
Save As backstage area				*Save* OR *Save As*	
Save As dialog box					F12
save document				*Save*	Ctrl + S
show white space					
Spelling & Grammar	Review, Proofing				F7
Tell Me feature	*Tell Me* text box				Alt + Q
Thesaurus	Review, Proofing				Shift + F7
undo an action					Ctrl + Z
Word Options dialog box				*Options*	

Workbook ▶ Section study tools and assessment activities are available in the *Workbook* ebook. These resources are designed to help you further develop and demonstrate mastery of the skills learned in this section.

Word

Formatting Characters and Paragraphs

Data Files — Before beginning section work, copy the WordS2 folder to your storage medium and then make WordS2 the active folder.

Skills

- Apply fonts and font effects
- Apply formatting with Format Painter
- Repeat a command
- Align text in paragraphs
- Indent text
- Change line spacing
- Change paragraph spacing
- Find and replace formatting
- Create bulleted and numbered lists

- Insert symbols
- Insert special characters
- Set tabs and tabs with leaders
- Apply borders and shading to text
- Apply a page border
- Apply styles and style sets
- Apply themes

Precheck — Check your current skills to help focus your study of the skills taught in this section.

Projects Overview

Edit and format documents on Oslo, Norway, and Petersburg, Alaska; format a document on traveling by train in Europe; and format documents on vacation packages in Oregon and Nevada and cross-country skiing vacation packages.

Prepare a letter to the chair of the Theatre Arts Division at Niagara Peninsula College requesting 20 theatre interns.

Prepare a movie distribution schedule.

SNAP If you are a SNAP user, launch the Precheck and Tutorials from your Assignments page.

Model Answers — Preview the model answers for an overview of the projects you will complete in the section activities.

Apply character formatting to text with buttons in the Font group on the Home tab. Formatting a document changes how the document displays and prints. The top row of the Font group contains options and buttons for changing the font and font size of text as well as changing text case and clearing formatting. The bottom row contains buttons for applying formatting to text such as bold, italics, underlining, strikethrough, subscript, superscript, text effects, highlighting, and font color. Microsoft Word has taken some commonly used commands and placed them on the Mini toolbar. When you select text, the Mini toolbar displays above the selected text. The Mini toolbar disappears when you move the mouse pointer away from it.

What You Will Do   You have been asked to improve the appearance of a document on Oslo, Norway, by applying a different font and various font effects to the text.

Tutorial
Applying Font Formatting Using the Font Group

Tutorial
Applying Font Formatting Using the Mini Toolbar

Tutorial
Highlighting Text

1 Open **FCTOslo.docx** and then save it with the name **2-FCTOslo**.

2 Select the words *Oslo, Norway* and then click the Bold button B in the Font group on the Home tab.

3 With *Oslo, Norway* still selected, click the Change Case button Aa ▾ in the Font group and then click *UPPERCASE* at the drop-down list.

> Use options at the Change Case drop-down list to specify the case of selected text.

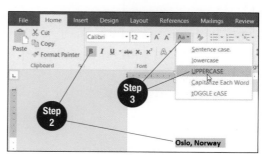

4 With *OSLO, NORWAY* still selected, click the Text Effects and Typography button A ▾ and then click the *Fill - White, Outline - Accent 1, Shadow* option at the drop-down gallery (fourth column, first row).

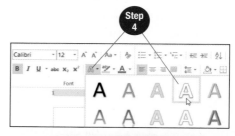

5 Select *History* and then click the Underline button U ▾ in the Font group.

6 Select and then underline the remaining headings: *Population*; *Commerce and Industry*; *Climate*; *Holiday, Sport, and Leisure*; and *Sightseeing Tours*.

7 Select the words *Viking Age* in the first paragraph below the *History* heading and then click the Italic button I on the Mini toolbar above the selected text.

> The Mini toolbar displays above selected text. The toolbar disappears when you move the mouse pointer away from it.

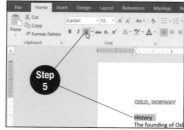

8 Select the words *Catholic Middle Ages* in the first paragraph and then click the Italic button on the Mini toolbar.

9 Select the entire document by clicking the Select button in the Editing group on the Home tab and then clicking *Select All* at the drop-down list.

10 Click the *Font* option box arrow in the Font group. Hover the mouse pointer over various typefaces in the drop-down gallery and notice how the text in the document reflects the selected font.

> This feature is referred to as *live preview*. It provides you with an opportunity to see how the document will appear with text formatting applied before you actually apply it.

11 Scroll down the gallery and then click *Constantia*.

12 Click the *Font Size* option box arrow and then click *11* in the drop-down gallery.

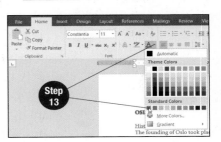

13 Click the Font Color button arrow and then click the *Dark Red* color option (first option in the *Standard Colors* section).

14 Deselect the text by clicking anywhere in the document.

15 You want to identify specific text for review by colleagues so you decide to highlight the text. To do this, click the Text Highlight Color button arrow in the Font group and then click the *Yellow* color option at the drop-down list. Select the first sentence in the second paragraph (the sentence that begins *Oslo's population was substantially reduced*).

> When you click the Text Highlight Color button, the mouse pointer displays with a highlighter pen attached. Highlighting stays on until you click the Text Highlight Color button again.

16 Select the first sentence in the *Population* paragraph to highlight it and then click the Text Highlight Color button to turn it off.

17 Remove the text highlighting by pressing Ctrl + A (this selects the entire document), clicking the Text Highlight Color button arrow, and then clicking *No Color* at the drop-down list.

18 Save **2-FCTOslo.docx**.

Check Your Work Compare your work to the model answer to ensure that you have completed the activity correctly.

In Addition

Using Typefaces

A typeface is a set of characters with a common design and shape. It can be decorative or plain and either monospaced or proportional. Word refers to typeface as *fonts*. A monospaced typeface allots the same amount of horizontal space for each character, while a proportional typeface allots a varying amount of space for each character. Proportional typefaces are divided into two main categories: *serif* and *sans serif*. A serif is a small line at the end of a character stroke. Consider using a serif typeface for text-intensive documents because the serifs help move the reader's eyes across the page. Use a sans serif typeface for headings, headlines, and advertisements.

In addition to buttons in the Font group, you can apply font formatting with options at the Font dialog box. Display the Font dialog box by clicking the Font group dialog box launcher. With options at this dialog box, you can change the font, font size, and font style; change the font color; choose an underline style; and apply formatting effects. Once you apply formatting to text, you can copy that formatting to different locations in the document using the Format Painter. If you apply formatting to text in a document and then want to repeat the formatting for other text, use the Repeat command. Repeat a command by pressing the F4 function key or Ctrl + Y.

Tutorial
Applying Font Formatting Using the Font Dialog Box

Tutorial
Formatting with Format Painter

Tutorial
Repeating the Last Action

What You Will Do   The changes you made to the Oslo document have enhanced the readability and appearance of the text. Now you will turn your attention to the headings.

1 With **2-FCTOslo.docx** open, press Ctrl + Home to move the insertion point to the beginning of the document and then select the entire document by pressing Ctrl + A.

2 Click the Font group dialog box launcher.

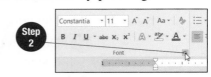

3 At the Font dialog box, click *Cambria* in the *Font* list box (you will need to scroll up the list box to display this option) and then click *12* in the *Size* list box.

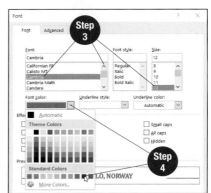

4 Click the *Font color* option box arrow and then click the *Dark Blue* color option (ninth option in the *Standard Colors* section).

5 Click OK to close the dialog box.

6 Select the heading *History* and then click the Font group dialog box launcher.

7 Click *Candara* in the *Font* list box (you will need to scroll down the list box to display this option), click *Bold* in the *Font style* list box, and then click *14* in the *Size* list box (you will need to scroll down the list box to display this option).

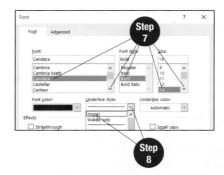

8 Click the *Underline style* option box arrow and then click *(none)* at the drop-down list.

9 Click OK to close the dialog box.

10 Click anywhere in the heading *History* and then double-click the Format Painter button in the Clipboard group on the Home tab.

When Format Painter is active, the mouse pointer displays with a paintbrush attached. Click the Format Painter button to apply formatting to one location only. Double-click the Format Painter button to apply formatting to more than one location.

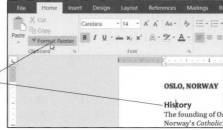

11 Select the title *OSLO, NORWAY*.

> With Format Painter active, selecting text applies formatting. Selecting the title removed the text effect and applied the same formatting that you applied to the *History* heading.

12 Scroll down the document and then click anywhere in the word *Population*.

> When using Format Painter, apply formatting to a single word by clicking anywhere in the word. To apply formatting to more than one word at a time, select the text.

13 Select individually each of the headings: *Commerce and Industry*; *Climate*; *Holiday, Sport, and Leisure*; and *Sightseeing Tours*.

14 Click the Format Painter button to turn off Format Painter.

15 Select the last sentence in the document (the sentence that begins *All tours by boat*) and then click the Font group dialog box launcher.

16 At the Font dialog box, click the *Small caps* check box in the *Effects* section to insert a check mark.

17 Click OK to close the dialog box.

18 Select the text *Tour 1: Mini Cruise* and then press F4.

> Pressing F4 repeats the previous command and applies the small caps effect to the selected text.

19 Select the text *Tour 2: Fjord Cruise* and then press F4. Select the text *Tour 3: Fjord Cruise with Dinner* and then press F4. Select the text *Tour 4: Selected Oslo Sightseeing* and then press F4.

> You can also repeat a command with the keyboard shortcut Ctrl + Y.

20 Press Ctrl + Home to move the insertion point to the beginning of the document, select the heading *OSLO, NORWAY,* and then change the font size to 16 points.

21 Save **2-FCTOslo.docx**.

Check Your Work Compare your work to the model answer to ensure that you have completed the activity correctly.

In Addition

Using Font Keyboard Shortcuts

Along with buttons in the Font group and the Font dialog box, you can apply character formatting with the following keyboard shortcuts:

Font Group Button	Keyboard Shortcut		Font Group Button	Keyboard Shortcut
Font	Ctrl + Shift + F		Bold	Ctrl + B
Font Size	Ctrl + Shift + P		Italic	Ctrl + I
Increase Font Size	Ctrl + Shift + >		Underline	Ctrl + U
Decrease Font Size	Ctrl + Shift + <		Subscript	Ctrl + =
Change Case	Shift + F3		Superscript	Ctrl + Shift + +

Activity 2.3 Aligning Text

Paragraphs of text in a document are aligned at the left margin by default. This default alignment can be changed to center, right, or justified. Change paragraph alignment with buttons in the Paragraph group on the Home tab, with the *Alignment* option at the Paragraph dialog box, or with keyboard shortcuts. Text alignment can be changed before you type a paragraph or you can change the alignment of an existing paragraph or group of paragraphs.

Tutorial
Changing Paragraph Alignment

What You Will Do You will improve the appearance of the Oslo document by changing the text alignment of specific paragraphs in the document.

1 With **2-FCTOslo.docx** open, position the insertion point anywhere in the title *OSLO, NORWAY.*

2 Click the Center button ☰ in the Paragraph group on the Home tab.

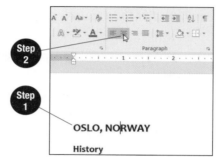

3 Select from the middle of the first paragraph of text below the *History* heading to somewhere in the middle of the third paragraph of text.

> Entire paragraphs do not have to be selected to change the alignment, only a portion of each paragraph.

4 Click the Justify button ☰ in the Paragraph group.

5 Press Ctrl + End to move the insertion point to the end of the document.

6 Click the Align Right button ☰ in the Paragraph group.

7 Type your first and last names, press Shift + Enter key, and then type First Choice Travel.

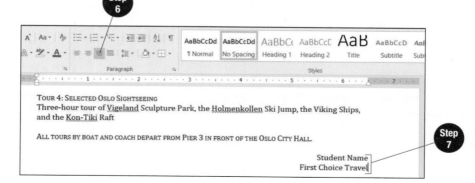

8 Click any character in the sentence above your first and last names (the sentence that begins *ALL TOURS BY BOAT AND COACH...*).

9 Click the Paragraph group dialog box launcher.

Clicking the Paragraph group dialog box launcher displays the Paragraph dialog box with the Indents and Spacing tab selected. Use the *Alignment* option box in the *General* section to change text alignment in the document.

10 At the Paragraph dialog box, click the *Alignment* option box arrow.

11 Click the *Centered* option at the drop-down list.

The *Alignment* option box at the Paragraph dialog box provides another method for changing paragraph alignment.

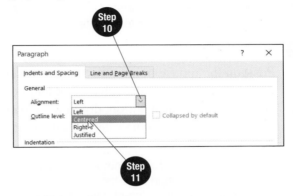

12 Click OK to close the Paragraph dialog box and apply center alignment to the sentence.

13 Move the insertion point to the beginning of the document.

14 Select the three paragraphs of text below the *History* heading.

15 Click the Align Left button in the Paragraph group and then deselect the text.

16 Save **2-FCTOslo.docx**.

Check Your Work — Compare your work to the model answer to ensure that you have completed the activity correctly.

In Addition

Aligning Text with Keyboard Shortcuts

Align text with the following keyboard shortcuts:

Alignment	Keyboard Shortcut
Left	Ctrl + L
Center	Ctrl + E
Right	Ctrl + R
Justified	Ctrl + J

Activity 2.4 Indenting Text

A paragraph of text in a document can be indented. For example, you can indent the first line of text in a paragraph, all lines of text in a paragraph, or the second and subsequent lines of a paragraph (called a *hanging indent*). Several methods are available for indenting text, including buttons in the Paragraph group on the Home tab and the Layout tab, markers on the horizontal ruler, options at the Paragraph dialog box with the Indents and Spacing tab selected, and keyboard shortcuts.

What You Will Do   You will improve the appearance of the Oslo document by changing the indent of specific paragraphs of text.

1. Select the three paragraphs of text below the *History* heading.

2. Position the mouse pointer on the Left Indent marker on the horizontal ruler, click and hold down the left mouse button, drag the marker to the 0.5-inch mark on the ruler, and then release the mouse button.

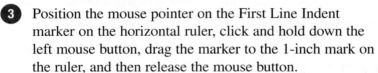

   If the horizontal ruler is not visible, click the View tab and then click the *Ruler* check box in the Show group to insert a check mark. The ruler indent markers are shown in Figure 2.1. To precisely position a marker on the ruler, hold down the Alt key while dragging the marker.

3. Position the mouse pointer on the First Line Indent marker on the horizontal ruler, click and hold down the left mouse button, drag the marker to the 1-inch mark on the ruler, and then release the mouse button.

4. Position the mouse pointer on the Right Indent marker on the ruler, click and hold down the left mouse button, drag the marker to the 6-inch mark on the ruler, and then release the mouse button.

5. Click anywhere in the paragraph below the *Population* heading and then click the Layout tab.

6. In the *Indent* section of the Paragraph group, click in the *Left* measurement box and then type 0.5.

7. Click the *Right* measurement box up arrow until *0.5"* displays.

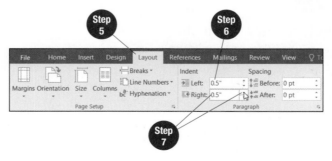

8 Click anywhere in the paragraph below the *Commerce and Industry* heading.

9 Click the Paragraph group dialog box launcher.

10 At the Paragraph dialog box, select the number in the *Left* measurement box in the *Indentation* section and then type 0.5. Select the number in the *Right* measurement box in the *Indentation* section and then type 0.5.

11 Click OK to close the Paragraph dialog box.

12 Click anywhere in the paragraph below the *Climate* heading and then press F4.

13 Click anywhere in the paragraph below the *Holiday, Sport, and Leisure* heading and then press F4.

14 Select the text below the *Sightseeing Tours* heading except the right-aligned text and then press F4.

15 Select the three paragraphs below the *History* heading and then click the Paragraph group dialog box launcher.

16 At the Paragraph dialog box, click the *Special* option box arrow in the *Indentation* section and then click *Hanging* at the drop-down list.

17 Click OK to close the Paragraph dialog box.

18 Save **2-FCTOslo.docx**.

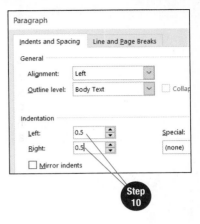

Step 10

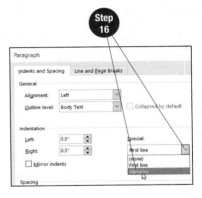

Step 16

Figure 2.1 Ruler Indent Markers

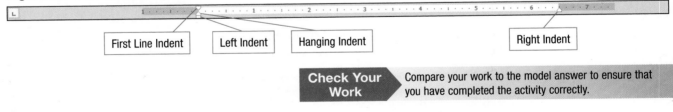

First Line Indent | Left Indent | Hanging Indent | Right Indent

Check Your Work   Compare your work to the model answer to ensure that you have completed the activity correctly.

In Addition

Indenting Text with Keyboard Shortcuts
Indent text with the following keyboard shortcuts:

Indentation	Keyboard Shortcut
Indent text from left margin	Ctrl + M
Decrease indent from left margin	Ctrl + Shift + M
Create a hanging indent	Ctrl + T
Remove hanging indent	Ctrl + Shift + T

Activity 2.5 Changing Line and Paragraph Spacing

By default, line spacing is set at 1.08. This default line spacing can be changed with the Line and Paragraph Spacing button in the Paragraph group on the Home tab, keyboard shortcuts, or with the *Line spacing* and *At* options at the Paragraph dialog box. Control spacing above and below paragraphs with options at the Line and Paragraph Spacing button drop-down list, the *Before* and *After* text boxes in the *Spacing* section in the Paragraph group on the Layout tab, or with the *Before* and *After* options in the *Spacing* section of the Paragraph dialog box with the Indents and Spacing tab selected.

What You Will Do The Oslo document project deadline is soon. However, you have time to make a few spacing changes in the document before printing the final version.

Tutorial
Changing Line Spacing

Tutorial
Changing Spacing Before and After Paragraphs

Tutorial
Keeping Text Together

1. With **2-FCTOslo.docx** open, select the entire document by pressing Ctrl + A.

2. Click the Home tab, click the Line and Paragraph Spacing button in the Paragraph group, and then click *1.5* at the drop-down list.

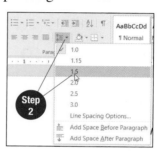

3. Deselect the text and then scroll through the document.

4. After viewing the document with 1.5 line spacing, you decide to decrease the line spacing to 1.2 (which is not an option available at the Line and Paragraph Spacing button drop-down list). To begin, press Ctrl + A to select the entire document.

5. Click the Line and Paragraph Spacing button and then click *Line Spacing Options* at the drop-down list.

   You can also display the Paragraph dialog box by clicking the Paragraph group dialog box launcher.

6. Type 1.2 in the *At* measurement box in the *Spacing* section of the Paragraph dialog box.

   The Paragraph dialog box also contains a *Line spacing* option box. Click the *Line spacing* option box arrow to display a drop-down list with spacing choices.

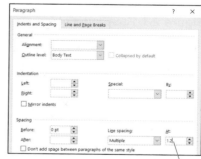

7. Click OK to close the dialog box and then deselect the text.

8. Select the line of text beginning *Tour 1: Mini Cruise* through *Tour 4: Selected Oslo Sightseeing* and the two lines that follow.

9. Click the Line and Paragraph Spacing button and then click *1.0* at the drop-down list.

   Choosing this option changes the line spacing to single for the selected paragraphs of text. You can also change line spacing with keyboard shortcuts. Press Ctrl + 1 to change to single spacing, Ctrl + 2 to change to double spacing, and Ctrl + 5 to change to 1.5 line spacing.

10. Click anywhere in the last sentence (the sentence that begins *All tours by boat*).

11. Click the Line and Paragraph Spacing button and then click *Add Space Before Paragraph*.

    This inserts 12 points of space above the sentence.

In Brief

Change Line Spacing
1. Click Line and Paragraph Spacing button.
2. Click line spacing option.
OR
1. Click Line and Paragraph Spacing button.
2. Click *Line Spacing Options*.
3. Type line spacing in *At* text box.
4. Click OK.

12 Press Ctrl + Home to move the insertion point to the beginning of the document, click anywhere in the *History* heading, and then click the Paragraph group dialog box launcher.

13 At the Paragraph dialog box, click the *After* measurement box up arrow.

Clicking the up arrow changes the measurement to 6 points.

14 Click OK to close the dialog box.

15 Click anywhere in the *Population* heading, click the Layout tab, and then click the *After* measurement box up arrow in the *Spacing* section of the Paragraph group.

Clicking the up arrow changes the measurement to 6 points.

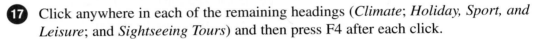

16 Click anywhere in the *Commerce and Industry* heading and then press F4.

Pressing F4 repeats the paragraph spacing command.

17 Click anywhere in each of the remaining headings (*Climate*; *Holiday, Sport, and Leisure*; and *Sightseeing Tours*) and then press F4 after each click.

18 You decide that you want to remove the hanging indent from the paragraphs in the *History* section. To do this, select the three paragraphs of text below the *History* heading and then press Ctrl + Shift + T.

Ctrl + Shift + T is the keyboard shortcut to remove hanging indent formatting.

19 Scroll down the page and notice that the *Climate* heading displays at the bottom of the first page while the paragraph that follows the heading displays at the top of the second page. You want to keep the heading with the paragraph of text. Begin by clicking anywhere in the *Climate* heading and then clicking the Paragraph group dialog box launcher.

20 At the Paragraph dialog box, click the Line and Page Breaks tab and then click the *Keep with next* check box to insert a check mark.

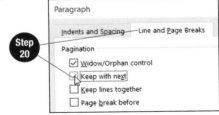

21 Click OK to close the Paragraph dialog box.

22 Save **2-FCTOslo.docx**.

Check Your Work Compare your work to the model answer to ensure that you have completed the activity correctly.

In Addition

Changing Spacing Above or Below Paragraphs

Spacing above or below paragraphs is added in points. For example, to add 9 points of spacing below selected paragraphs, click the Layout tab or display the Paragraph dialog box with the Indents and Spacing tab selected. Select the current measurement in the *After* measurement box and then type 9. You can also click the up or down arrows to increase or decrease the amount of spacing before or after paragraphs.

With options at the Find and Replace dialog box with the Replace tab selected, you can search for specific formatting or characters containing specific formatting and replace it with other formatting or characters. Click the More button to expand the options in the Find and Replace dialog box. Use the Format button at the expanded dialog box to specify the type of formatting to find and also the type of replacement formatting.

FIRST CHOICE TRAVEL

What You Will Do   After reviewing the Oslo document, you decide that the headings would look better set in a different font and font color. You decide to use the Find and Replace dialog box to find text with specific formatting applied and replace the text with different formatting.

Tutorial
Finding and Replacing Formatting

1   With **2-FCTOslo.docx** open, press Ctrl + Home to move the insertion point to the beginning of the document.

2   The headings in the document are set in 14-point Candara bold and dark blue color. You decide to replace that formatting with 14-point Arial bold italic and orange color. To begin, click the Replace button in the Editing group on the Home tab.

3   At the Find and Replace dialog box, press the Delete key. (This deletes any text in the *Find what* text box.)

4   Click the More button. (If a check mark displays in the *Find all word forms* check box, click the check box to remove the check mark.)

5   Click the Format button at the bottom of the dialog box and then click *Font* at the drop-down list.

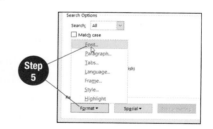

6   At the Find Font dialog box, click *Candara* in the *Font* list box, click *Bold* in the *Font style* list box, click *14* in the *Size* list box, click the *Font color* option box arrow, and then click *Dark Blue* in the *Standard Colors* section.

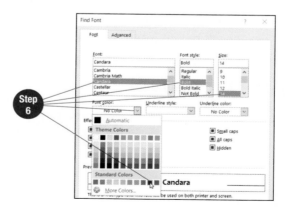

7   Click OK to close the dialog box.

8 At the Find and Replace dialog box, select and then delete any text in the *Replace with* text box.

9 With the insertion point in the *Replace with* text box, click the Format button at the bottom of the dialog box and then click *Font* at the drop-down list.

10 At the Replace Font dialog box, click *Arial* in the *Font* list box, click *Bold Italic* in the *Font style* list box, click *14* in the *Size* list box, click the *Font color* option box arrow, and then click *Orange, Accent 2, Darker 50%* (sixth column, bottom row in the *Theme Colors* section).

11 Click OK to close the dialog box.

12 At the Find and Replace dialog box, click the Replace All button.

13 At the message telling you that the search of the document is complete and six replacements were made, click OK.

14 With the Find and Replace dialog box open and the insertion point positioned in the *Find what* text box, click the No Formatting button at the bottom of the dialog box.

15 Click in the *Replace with* text box and then click the No Formatting button.

16 Click the Less button to reduce the size of the Find and Replace dialog box and then close the dialog box.

17 Save, print, and then close **2-FCTOslo.docx**.

Check Your Work — Compare your work to the model answer to ensure that you have completed the activity correctly.

In Addition

Revealing Formatting

Display formatting applied to specific text in a document at the Reveal Formatting task pane. The task pane displays font, paragraph, and section formatting applied to text where the insertion point is positioned or to selected text. Press Shift + F1 to display the Reveal Formatting task pane. Generally, a black triangle precedes *Font* and *Paragraph* in the task pane and a white triangle precedes *Section* in the *Formatting of selected text* section. Click the black triangle to hide any items below a heading and click the white triangle to reveal items. Some items in the Reveal Formatting task pane are hyperlinks. For example, click the FONT hyperlink to display the Font dialog box. Use these hyperlinks to make changes to the document formatting.

Comparing Formatting

Along with displaying formatting applied to text, you can use the Reveal Formatting task pane to compare formatting of two text selections to determine how it is different. To compare formatting, display the Reveal Formatting task pane and then select the first instance of formatting to be compared. Click the *Compare to another selection* check box to insert a check mark and then select the second instance of formatting to compare. Any differences between the two selections will display in the *Formatting differences* list box.

If you want to draw the reader's attention to a list of items, consider inserting a bullet before each item using the Bullets button in the Paragraph group on the Home tab. If the list of items is in a sequence, consider inserting numbers before each item with the Numbering button in the Paragraph group. Create multiple-level bulleted or numbered lists with options at the Multilevel List button drop-down list in the Paragraph group.

What You Will Do   First Choice Travel has created a new document on traveling in Europe by train. After reviewing the document, you decide to insert numbers and bullets before selected paragraphs to make the information easier to read.

Tutorial
Creating Numbered Lists

Tutorial
Creating Bulleted Lists

Tutorial
Creating Custom Bullets

Tutorial
Applying Multilevel List Numbering

1 Open **FCTRailTravel.docx** and then save it with the name **2-FCTRailTravel**.

2 Select text from the paragraph *Have your pass validated.* through the paragraph *Be at the right train station.* and then click the Numbering button in the Paragraph group on the Home tab.

3 Position the insertion point at the end of the second numbered paragraph (the paragraph that displays as *2. Protect your pass.*) and then press the Enter key.

Pressing the Enter key automatically inserts the number *3.* and renumbers the third paragraph to *4.*

4 Type Arrive 20 minutes before train departure time.

Numbering before paragraphs changes automatically when paragraphs of text are inserted and/or deleted.

5 Select text from the paragraph that begins *Free or discount transportation* through the paragraph that begins *Reduced rental rates with* and then click the Bullets button in the Paragraph group.

Clicking the Bullets button inserts a solid, round bullet before each paragraph. Other bullet options are available by clicking the Bullets button arrow.

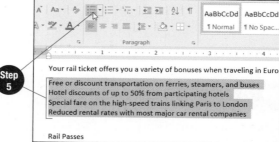

6 With the text still selected, replace the round bullet with a custom bullet. To begin, click the Bullets button arrow and then click *Define New Bullet* at the drop-down list.

7 At the Define New Bullet dialog box, click the Symbol button in the *Bullet character* section.

8 At the Symbol dialog box, click the *Font* option box arrow, type w, and then click *Webdings*.

9 Scroll to the end of the symbol list and then click the Earth symbol in the bottom row (as shown at the right; the location in the row may vary).

10 Click OK to close the Symbol dialog box.

11 Click OK to close the Define New Bullet dialog box.

12 Select the text from *Rail Passes* through *Greece-Italy*.

13 Click the Multilevel List button in the Paragraph group and then click the middle option in the top row of the *List Library* section.

> This applies multiple-level numbering to the selected text.

14 With the text still selected, change to bullets instead of numbers. To do this, click the Multilevel List button and then click the first option from the left in the middle row of the *List Library* section.

15 Deselect the text.

16 Save **2-FCTRailTravel.docx**.

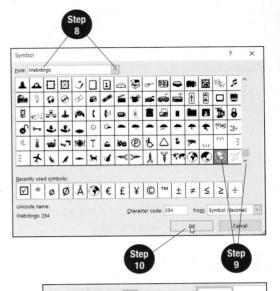

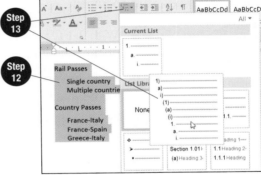

Check Your Work — Compare your work to the model answer to ensure that you have completed the activity correctly.

In Addition

Creating Numbered and/or Bulleted Text

If you type *1.* and then press the spacebar, Word indents the number approximately 0.25 inch and then hang indents the text in the paragraph approximately 0.5 inch from the left margin. When you press the Enter key after typing text, *2.* is inserted 0.25 inch from the left margin at the beginning of the next paragraph. Continue typing items and Word will continue numbering them. Press the Enter key two times to turn off numbering or click the Numbering button in the Paragraph group. Bulleted lists with hanging indents are automatically created when you begin a paragraph with the symbol *, > , or -. Type one of the symbols, press the spacebar, and the symbol bullet is inserted in the document. The type of bullet inserted depends on the type of character entered. For example, if you use the asterisk (*) symbol, a round bullet is inserted.

Turning Off Automatic Numbering and/or Bulleting

If you do not want automatic numbering or bulleting in a document, turn off the features at the AutoCorrect dialog box with the AutoFormat As You Type tab selected. To display this dialog box, click the File tab and then click *Options*. At the Word Options dialog box, click the *Proofing* option and then click the AutoCorrect Options button. At the AutoCorrect dialog box, click the AutoFormat As You Type tab. Click the *Automatic numbered lists* check box and/or *Automatic bulleted lists* check box to remove the check mark(s).

Insert special symbols such as é, ö, and Å with options at the Symbol palette or the Symbol dialog box. Display the Symbol palette by clicking the Insert tab and then clicking the Symbol button in the Symbols group. Click the desired symbol to insert it in the document. To display additional symbols, display the Symbol dialog box by clicking the Symbol button and then clicking the *More Symbols* option. Click the desired symbol at the dialog box, click the Insert button, and then click the Close button. At the Symbol dialog box with the Symbols tab selected, you can change the font and display different symbols. Click the Special Characters tab to display a list of special characters and the keyboard shortcuts to insert them.

What You Will Do   You have identified a few city names in the train travel document that need special letters in their spellings, as well as a special character you need to insert in the document.

Tutorial
Inserting Symbols

Tutorial
Inserting Special
Characters

1 With **2-FCTRailTravel.docx** open, move the insertion point to the end of the document and then select and delete the multiple-level bulleted text.

2 With the insertion point positioned at the end of the document a double space below the bulleted text, type the text shown in Figure 2.2 up to the *Å* in *Århus*.

3 Display the Symbol dialog by clicking the Insert tab, clicking the Symbol button Ω in the Symbols group, and then clicking the *More Symbols* option.

4 At the Symbol dialog box with the Symbols tab selected, click the *Font* option box arrow and then click *(normal text)* at the drop-down list. You may need to scroll up to see this option. Skip this step if *(normal text)* is already selected.

5 Scroll down the list box to somewhere between the seventh and ninth rows and then click the Å symbol.

6 Click the Insert button and then click the Close button.

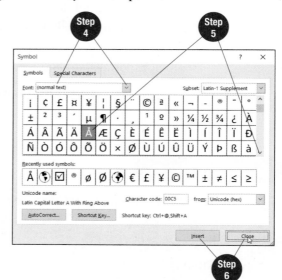

Figure 2.2 Steps 2–15

> Some companies offer outstanding reductions on transportation. For example, you can travel on the ferry in Denmark between Århus and Kalundborg and between Nyborg and Korsør at a 75% discount! ScanTravel, a travel company located in Stockholm, offers the StarPass® ticket that provides you with incredible discounts on travel by train, ferry, and bus in Sweden, Norway, and Denmark.

In Brief

Insert Symbol
1. Click Insert tab.
2. Click Symbol button.
3. Click *More Symbols*.
4. Click symbol.
5. Click Insert button.
6. Click Close button.

Insert Special Character
1. Click Insert tab.
2. Click Symbol button.
3. Click *More Symbols*.
4. Click Special Characters tab.
5. Click character.
6. Click Insert button.
7. Click Close button.

7 Continue typing the text in Figure 2.2 up to the ø symbol. To insert the ø symbol, click the Symbol button and then click *More Symbols*.

8 At the Symbol dialog box, click the ø symbol (somewhere between the tenth and twelfth rows).

9 Click the Insert button and then click the Close button.

10 Continue typing the text up to the ® character.

11 To insert the ® character, click the Symbol button and then click *More Symbols*.

12 At the Symbol dialog box, click the Special Characters tab.

13 Click the ® character in the list box.

14 Click the Insert button.

15 Click the Close button.

16 Type the remaining text in Figure 2.2. Press the Enter key two times when you are finished.

17 Save **2-FCTRailTravel.docx**.

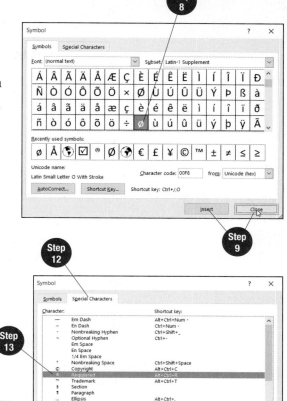

Check Your Work Compare your work to the model answer to ensure that you have completed the activity correctly.

In Addition

Inserting Symbols with Keyboard Shortcuts or Character Codes

Another method for inserting symbols in a document is to use keyboard shortcuts. Click a symbol at the Symbol dialog box and the keyboard shortcut displays toward the bottom of the dialog box. For example, click the ø symbol and the keyboard shortcut Ctrl + /,O displays toward the bottom of the dialog box. To insert the ø symbol in a document using the keyboard shortcut, hold down the Ctrl key and then press the / key. Release the Ctrl key and then press the O key. Not all symbols have a corresponding a keyboard shortcut. Each symbol has an identifying character code. If you know the character code of a symbol, type the code in the *Character code* text box in the Symbol dialog box. Click a symbol at the Symbol dialog box and symbol code displays in the *Character code* text box.

Inserting Symbols Using the Palette

When you click the Symbol button in the Symbols group, a drop-down palette displays with symbol choices. The palette displays the most recently used symbols. If the palette contains the symbol you need, click the symbol to insert it in the document.

Word offers a variety of default settings, including left tabs set every 0.5 inch. You can set, move, and delete your own tabs using the horizontal ruler. With a left tab, text aligns at the left edge of the tab. The other types of tabs that can be set on the horizontal ruler are center, right, decimal, and bar. The small button above the vertical ruler is called the Alignment button. Each time you click the Alignment button, a different tab or paragraph alignment symbol displays. To set a tab, display the desired tab symbol on the Alignment button and then click the horizontal ruler at the desired position.

What You Will Do   You have completed some additional research on train connections in Europe. You will add airport names to the train travel document.

Tutorial

Setting and Modifying Tabs on the Horizontal Ruler

1 With **2-FCTRailTravel.docx** open, make sure the insertion point is positioned a double space below the last paragraph of text in the document.

2 Type International Airports with Train Connections and then press the Enter key two times.

3 Make sure the left tab symbol ⌊ displays in the Alignment button above the vertical ruler. (If the left tab symbol does not display in the Alignment button, click the button until it does.)

> If tabs display on the horizontal ruler, clear the tabs by clicking the Clear All Formatting button 🅰 in the Font group on the Home tab.

4 Position the arrow pointer at the 1-inch mark on the horizontal ruler and then click the left mouse button.

5 Click the Alignment button to display the center tab symbol ⊥.

6 Position the arrow pointer at the 3.25-inch mark on the horizontal ruler and then click the left mouse button.

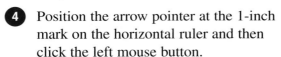

7 Click the Alignment button to display the right tab symbol ⌋.

8 Position the arrow pointer at the 5.5-inch mark on the horizontal ruler and then click the left mouse button.

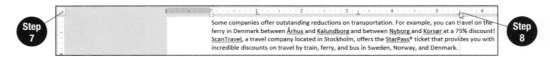

9 Type the text shown in Figure 2.3, pressing the Tab key before typing each tabbed entry. Make sure you press the Tab key before typing the entry in the first column and that you apply bold formatting to the text in the first row.

If your columns of text do not look similar to those in Figure 2.3, check to make sure you inserted the tab symbols at the correct locations on the horizontal ruler and that you pressed the Tab key before typing each entry in the first column.

10 After typing the last entry in the third column (*Fiumicino*), press the Enter key two times and then click the Clear All Formatting button in the Font group on the Home tab.

Clicking the Clear All Formatting button removes paragraph and character formatting. You can also remove paragraph formatting by pressing the keyboard shortcut Ctrl + Q and remove character formatting by pressing the keyboard shortcut Ctrl + spacebar.

11 Save **2-FCTRailTravel.docx**.

Figure 2.3 Step 9

Country	**City**	**Airport**
Austria	Vienna (Wein)	Schwechat
Belgium	Brussels	Nationaal
France	Paris	Orly
Germany	Berlin	Schoenefeld
Great Britain	London	Heathrow
Italy	Rome	Fiumicino

Check Your Work Compare your work to the model answer to ensure that you have completed the activity correctly.

In Addition

Moving a Tab

Move a tab on the horizontal ruler by positioning the mouse pointer on the tab symbol on the horizontal ruler, clicking and holding down the left mouse button, dragging the tab symbol to the new location on the ruler, and then releasing the mouse button.

Deleting a Tab

Delete a tab from the horizontal ruler by positioning the arrow pointer on the tab symbol, clicking and holding down the left mouse button, dragging the tab symbol down into the document screen, and then releasing the mouse button.

Setting a Decimal Tab

Set a decimal tab for column entries you want aligned at the decimal point. To set a decimal tab, click the Alignment button above the vertical ruler until the decimal tab symbol displays and then click the desired position on the horizontal ruler.

Left, right, center, and decimal tabs can be set with leaders. Leaders are useful for directing the reader's eyes across the page. Leaders can be periods, hyphens, or underlines. Set tabs with leaders by using options at the Tabs dialog box. To display the Tabs dialog box, click the Paragraph group dialog box launcher and then click the Tabs button at the Paragraph dialog box. At the Tabs dialog box, enter a tab position measurement, choose the type of tab, and then choose the type of leader.

FIRST CHOICE TRAVEL

What You Will Do   The information you found listing airports with train connections also includes schedule times. You will add this data to the train travel document.

Tutorial

Setting and Clearing Tabs at the Tabs Dialog Box

1. With **2-FCTRailTravel.docx** open, move the insertion point to the end of the document.

2. Click the Alignment button above the vertical ruler until the left tab symbol displays.

3. Position the arrow pointer at the 1-inch mark on the horizontal ruler and then click the left mouse button.

4. Click the Alignment button above the vertical ruler until the right tab symbol displays.

5. Position the arrow pointer at the 5.5-inch mark on the horizontal ruler and then click the left mouse button.

6. Type the headings shown in Figure 2.4 by pressing the Tab key, clicking the Bold button in the Font group, and then typing Airport.

7. Press the Tab key and then type Service.

8. Press the Enter key and then click the Clear All Formatting button to remove the bold formatting and the paragraph tab formatting.

9. Set a left tab and a right tab with leaders at the Tabs dialog box. To begin, click the Paragraph group dialog box launcher and then click the Tabs button in the lower left corner of the Paragraph dialog box.

   You can also display the Tabs dialog box by double-clicking any tab symbol on the horizontal ruler.

10. At the Tabs dialog box, select the *Left* option in the *Alignment* section of the dialog box, if necessary. With the insertion point positioned in the *Tab stop position* text box, type 1 and then click the Set button.

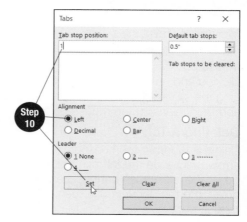

Step 10

Figure 2.4 Step 6, Step 7, and Step 14

Airport	Service
Schwechat	Train every 30 minutes
Nationaal	Train every 20 minutes
Orly...	RER train every 20 minutes
Schoenefeld	S-Bahn train every 30 minutes
Heathrow.......................................	LT train every 10 minutes
Fiumicino....................................	Train every 10 to 20 minutes

11 Type 5.5 in the *Tab stop position* text box, click the *Right* option in the *Alignment* section of the dialog box, and then click the *2.....* option in the *Leader* section of the dialog box.

12 Click the Set button.

13 Click OK to close the dialog box.

14 Type the remaining text shown in Figure 2.4, making sure you press the Tab key before typing the text in each column.

> If your columns of text do no look similar to those in Figure 2.4, check to make sure you inserted the tab symbols at the correct measurements and that you pressed the Tab key before typing each entry in the first column.

15 Press Ctrl + Home to move the insertion point to the beginning of the document.

16 Select the four numbered paragraphs.

17 With the paragraphs selected, click the Bullets button arrow in the Paragraph group and then click the Earth bullet in the *Bullet Library* section. (The Earth bullet is the bullet you selected in Activity 2.6.) If this bullet is not available at the drop-down list, complete steps similar to those in Activity 2.7, Steps 6 through 11, to select and apply the Earth bullet.

18 Save **2-FCTRailTravel.docx**.

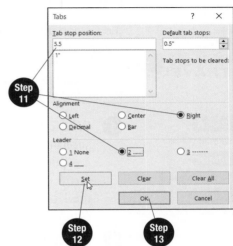

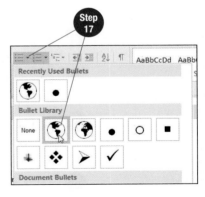

Check Your Work — Compare your work to the model answer to ensure that you have completed the activity correctly.

In Addition

Clearing Tabs at the Tabs Dialog Box

At the Tabs dialog box, you can clear an individual tab or all tabs. To clear all tabs, click the Clear All button. To clear an individual tab, specify the tab position and then click the Clear button.

Insert a border around text and/or apply shading to text in a paragraph or selected text with the Borders button and the Shading button in the Paragraph group on the Home tab or at the Borders and Shading dialog box. At the Borders and Shading dialog box with the Borders tab selected, specify the border type, style, color, and width. Click the Shading tab and the dialog box displays options for choosing a fill color and pattern style. Click the Page Border tab and the dialog box displays options for applying a page border. You can also access the Borders and Shading dialog box with the Page Border tab selected by clicking the Design tab and then clicking the Page Borders button in the Page Background group.

What You Will Do   To highlight certain information in the First Choice Travel train travel document, you will apply a border to selected text and apply border and shading formatting to the column text. You will also apply a page border to add visual appeal.

Tutorial
Applying Borders

Tutorial
Applying Shading

Tutorial
Inserting a Page Border

1. With **2-FCTRailTravel.docx** open, make sure the first four bulleted paragraphs are selected, click the Borders button arrow ⊞ ▾ in the Paragraph group on the Home tab, and then click *Outside Borders* at the drop-down gallery.

2. Select the second four bulleted paragraphs of text and then click the Borders button in the Paragraph group.

   This applies the outside border since that is the last border option you selected.

3. Select from the column headings *Country*, *City*, and *Airport* through the line of text containing the column entries *Italy*, *Rome*, and *Fiumicino*.

4. Click the Borders button arrow and then click *Borders and Shading* at the drop-down gallery.

5. At the Borders and Shading dialog box with the Borders tab selected, click the *Box* option in the *Setting* section.

6. Click the down arrow at the right side of the *Style* list box until the first double-line option displays and then click the double-line option.

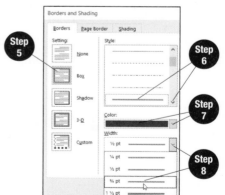

7. Click the *Color* option box arrow and then click the *Blue, Accent 1, Darker 50%* color option (fifth column, bottom row in the *Theme Colors* section).

8. Click the *Width* option box arrow and then click *¾ pt* at the drop-down list.

9. Click the Shading tab, click the *Fill* option box arrow, and then click the *Blue, Accent 1, Lighter 80%* color option (fifth column, second row in the *Theme Colors* section).

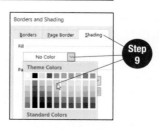

In Brief

Apply Borders
1. Select text.
2. Click Borders button arrow.
3. Click option.
OR
1. Selext text.
2. Click Borders button arrow.
3. Click *Borders and Shading*.
4. Choose border(s).
5. Click OK.

Apply Shading
1. Select text.
2. Click Borders button arrow.
3. Click *Borders and Shading*.
4. Click Shading tab.
5. Choose shading and/or pattern.
6. Click OK.

Insert Page Border
1. Click Borders button arrow.
2. Click *Borders and Shading*.
3. Click Page Border tab.
4. Choose options.
5. Click OK.
OR
1. Click Design tab.
2. Click Page Borders button.
3. Choose options.
4. Click OK.

10 Click OK to close the dialog box.

11 Add the same border and shading to the other columns of text by selecting from the column headings *Airport* and *Service* through the line of text containing the column entries *Fiumicino* and *Train every 10 to 20 minutes* and then pressing F4.

12 Apply shading to the title by positioning the insertion point in the text *Traveling in Europe by Train*, clicking the Shading button arrow , and then clicking the *Blue, Accent 1, Lighter 60%* color option (fifth column, third row in the *Theme Colors* section).

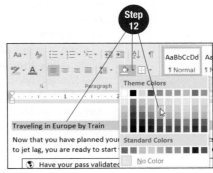

13 Insert a page border in the document. To begin, click the Borders button arrow and then click *Borders and Shading* at the drop-down list.

14 At the Borders and Shading dialog box, click the Page Border tab.

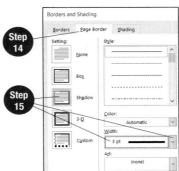

15 Click the *Shadow* option in the *Setting* section, click the *Width* option box arrow, and then click *3 pt* at the drop-down list.

16 Click OK to close the dialog box.

17 Change the page border to an art image. To begin, click the Design tab and then click the Page Borders button in the Page Background group.

18 At the Borders and Shading dialog box with the Page Border tab selected, click the *Box* option in the *Setting* section.

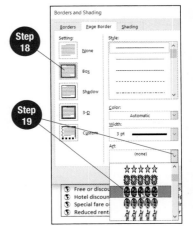

19 Click the *Art* option box arrow, scroll down the list until the globe art images display, and then click the first set of globe images as shown at the right.

20 Select the number in the *Width* measurement box and then type 10.

21 Click OK to close the dialog box.

22 Save **2-FCTRailTravel.docx**.

Check Your Work Compare your work to the model answer to ensure that you have completed the activity correctly.

In Addition

Applying Borders

The Borders and Shading dialog box with the Borders tab or the Page Border tab selected contains a Preview area you can use to insert borders at specfic locations. A diagram displays in the Preview area and you can click the sides, top, or bottom of the diagram to insert or remove a border line. Buttons display around the diagram that you can also use to apply borders.

A Word document is based on a template that applies default formatting such as 11-point Calibri font, line spacing of 1.08, and 8 points of spacing after each paragraph. You can change these default formats with buttons and options on the ribbon and also with styles. A style is a set of formatting instructions you can apply to text. To apply a predesigned style, click the desired style in the styles gallery in the Styles group on the Home tab. Click the More Styles button at the right side of the styles gallery to display a drop-down gallery of additional styles. Word groups styles that apply similar formatting into style sets. Style sets are available in the Document Formatting group on the Design tab. If you choose a different style set, the styles in the Styles group on the Home tab change to reflect the currently selected style set. A style set changes the formatting applied by styles. In addition to a style set, you can also apply formatting to a document with a theme. A theme is a set of formatting choices that includes a color theme (a set of colors), a font theme (a set of heading and body text fonts), and an effects theme (a set of lines and fill effects). Apply a theme with the Themes button in the Document Formatting group on the Design tab. Customize a theme (or style set) with the Colors, Fonts, and Effects buttons.

What You Will Do   To further enhance the train travel document, you decide to apply styles, a different style set, and a theme to the document.

Tutorial
Applying Styles and Style Sets

Tutorial
Applying and Modifying a Theme

1. With **2-FCTRailTravel.docx** open, press Ctrl + Home to move the insertion point to the beginning of the document.

2. Click anywhere in the title *Traveling in Europe by Train* and then click the *Heading 1* style in the styles gallery on the Home tab.

   > The Heading 1 style in the default style set changes the font size and font color and adds 12 points of spacing above the title. Applying the heading style also removes the shading you inserted in the previous activity.

Step 2

3. Click anywhere in the heading *Rail Ticket Bonuses* and then click the *Heading 2* style in the Styles group.

4. Click anywhere in the heading *International Airports with Train Connections* and then click the *Heading 2* style.

5. Apply a different style set by clicking the Design tab, clicking the More Style Sets button at the right of the style sets gallery in the Document Formatting group, and then clicking *Lines (Stylish)*.

Step 5

6. Apply a paragraph spacing option so the text fits on one page by clicking the Paragraph Spacing button 📝 in the Document Formatting group and then clicking *Compact* at the drop-down gallery.

   > Display the paragraph and line formatting applied by a paragraph spacing option by hovering the mouse over the option at the drop-down gallery.

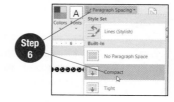

Step 6

7 Apply a theme by clicking the Themes button in the Document Formatting group and then clicking the *Retrospect* option.

8 Change the colors applied by the theme by clicking the Colors button in the Document Formatting group and then clicking the *Green* option at the drop-down gallery.

9 Change the fonts applied by the theme by clicking the Fonts button in the Document Formatting group and then clicking the *Corbel* option at the drop-down gallery.

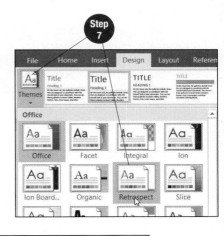

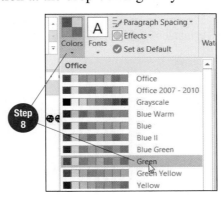

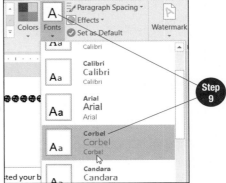

10 Select the title *Traveling in Europe by Train*, change the font size to 24 points, and then change the paragraph alignment to center.

11 Save, print, and then close **2-FCTRailTravel.docx**.

Check Your Work Compare your work to the model answer to ensure that you have completed the activity correctly.

In Addition

Applying the No Spacing Style

By default, a blank document contains line spacing of 1.08 and 8 points of spacing after paragraphs. The increase in line spacing and spacing after paragraphs creates more space between lines and is designed to make text easier to read on a computer screen. You can change the line spacing to 1.0 and remove the spacing after paragraphs by clicking the *No Spacing* style in the Styles group on the Home tab.

Collapsing and Expanding Headings

When you apply heading styles to text in a document, you can collapse text below the headings. By collapsing text, you can view the headings in your document and use the headings to easily navigate to specific locations. Collapse text in a document by clicking the gray triangle that displays when you hover the mouse pointer over text with a heading style applied. Expand a collapsed

document by clicking the white triangle before a heading with a style applied.

Applying Styles at the Styles Window

The Styles window provides additional styles. Display this window by clicking the Styles group dialog box launcher. The styles in the currently selected style set display in the window followed by a paragraph symbol (¶), indicating that the style applies paragraph formatting, or a character symbol (a), indicating that the style applies character formatting. If both characters display to the right of a style, the style applies both paragraph and character formatting. In addition to displaying styles that apply formatting, the Styles window also includes a Clear All style that clears all formatting from selected text.

Features Summary

Feature	Ribbon Tab, Group	Button	Keyboard Shortcut
1.5 line spacing	Home, Paragraph		Ctrl + 5
align left	Home, Paragraph		Ctrl + L
align right	Home, Paragraph		Ctrl + R
bold	Home, Font		Ctrl + B
borders	Home, Paragraph		
bullets	Home, Paragraph		
center	Home, Paragraph		Ctrl + E
change case	Home, Font		Shift + F3
clear all formatting	Home, Font		
clear character formatting			Ctrl + spacebar
clear paragraph formatting			Ctrl + Q
decrease font size	Home, Font		Ctrl + Shift + <
decrease indent	Home, Paragraph		Ctrl + Shift + M
double line spacing	Home, Paragraph		Ctrl + 2
Find and Replace dialog box with Replace tab selected	Home, Editing		Ctrl + H
font	Home, Font		Ctrl + Shift + F
font color	Home, Font		
Font dialog box	Home, Font		Ctrl + D
font size	Home, Font		Ctrl + Shift + P
Format Painter	Home, Clipboard		Ctrl + Shift + C
hanging indent	Home, Paragraph		Ctrl + T
highlight	Home, Font		
increase font size	Home, Font		Ctrl + Shift + >
increase indent	Home, Paragraph		Ctrl + M
insert symbol	Insert, Symbols		
italics	Home, Font		Ctrl + I
justify	Home, Paragraph		Ctrl + J

Features Summary

Feature	Ribbon Tab, Group	Button	Keyboard Shortcut
line and paragraph spacing	Home, Paragraph		
multilevel list	Home, Paragraph		
numbering	Home, Paragraph		
Paragraph dialog box	Home, Paragraph		
repeat a command			F4
remove hanging indent	Home, Paragraph		Ctrl + Shift + T
shading	Home, Paragraph		
single line spacing	Home, Paragraph		Ctrl + 1
spacing after	Layout, Paragraph		
spacing before	Layout, Paragraph		
styles	Home, Styles		
style sets	Design, Document Formatting		
subscript	Home, Font	x_2	Ctrl + =
superscript	Home, Font	x^2	Ctrl + Shift + +
Tabs dialog box	Home, Paragraph	, Tabs	
theme colors	Design, Document Formatting		
theme fonts	Design, Document Formatting	A	
themes	Design, Document Formatting		
underline	Home, Font	U	Ctrl + U

Workbook Section study tools and assessment activities are available in the *Workbook* ebook. These resources are designed to help you further develop and demonstrate mastery of the skills learned in this section.

Word

Formatting and Enhancing a Document

Data Files Before beginning section work, copy the WordS3 folder to your storage medium and then make WordS3 the active folder.

Skills

- Cut, copy, and paste text
- Use the Clipboard task pane to copy and paste items
- Change page margins, orientation, and size
- Insert a watermark, page color, and page border
- Insert page numbering
- Insert a header and footer
- Format a document in MLA style
- Insert sources and citations

- Create a works cited page
- Edit a source
- Use the Click and Type feature
- Vertically align text
- Insert, size, and move images
- Prepare an envelope and mailing labels

Precheck Check your current skills to help focus your study of the skills taught in this section.

Projects Overview

Edit and format documents on Thailand and Juneau, Alaska; prepare an announcement about a workshop on traveling on a budget; format a report on the Middleton Valley in MLA style; prepare envelopes and labels for mailing fact sheets and announcements.

Format reports in MLA style; format a costume rental agreement.

Prepare an announcement about a workshop on employment opportunities in the movie industry; add a picture watermark.

Create an announcement for weekend work; prepare labels.

Prepare an announcement about internship positions available at Marquee Productions; prepare labels for the college.

 **SNAP** If you are a SNAP user, launch the Precheck and Tutorials from your Assignments page.

Model Answers Preview the model answers for an overview of the projects you will complete in the section activities.

With the Cut, Copy, and Paste buttons in the Clipboard group on the Home tab, you can move and/or copy words, sentences, or entire sections of text to other locations in a document. You can cut and paste text or copy and paste text within the same document or between documents. Specify the formatting of pasted text with the Paste Options button or options at the Paste Special dialog box.

What You Will Do   You are working on a First Choice Travel document containing information on Thailand. You decide that some of the text in the document should be reorganized, and you also decide to add additional information to the document.

Tutorial
Cutting, Copying, and Pasting Text

Tutorial
Using the Paste Options Button

Tutorial
Using Paste Special

1. Open **FCTThailand.docx** and then save it with the name **3-FCTThailand**.

2. Move the *Attractions* section below the *Traveling in Thailand* section. Begin by selecting the *Attractions* heading and the paragraph of text that follows it.

3. Click the Cut button in the Clipboard group on the Home tab.

   Clicking the Cut button places the text in a special location within Word called the *Clipboard*.

4. Move the insertion point to the beginning of the *Accommodations* heading and then click the Paste button in the Clipboard group on the Home tab.

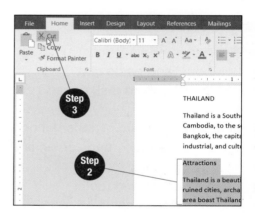

5. Open **FCTThaiStats.docx**.

   You will copy text from this document and paste it in the Thailand information document.

6. Select the *Points of Interest* heading and the four lines of text below it and then click the Copy button in the Clipboard group.

7. Click the Word button on the taskbar and then click the **3-FCTThailand.docx** thumbnail.

8. Position the insertion point at the beginning of the heading *Passports/Visas* and then click the Paste button in the Clipboard group.

   A Paste Options button ⌧ (Ctrl) ▾ displays below the pasted text. Click this button and a drop-down gallery of buttons displays. Use these buttons to specify the formatting of the pasted text. By default, the Keep Source Formatting button (first button from the left) is selected. With this button selected, text is pasted with the formatting from the source document. You can also click the Merge Formatting button (middle button) to merge formatting with the destination formatting or click the Keep Text Only button (third button) to paste only the text and not the formatting.

In Brief

Cut and Paste Text
1. Select text.
2. Click Cut button in Clipboard group.
3. Position insertion point.
4. Click Paste button.

Copy and Paste Text
1. Select text.
2. Click Copy button.
3. Position insertion point.
4. Click Paste button.

Use Paste Special
1. Cut or copy text.
2. Click Paste button arrow.
3. Click *Paste Special*.
4. Click format in *As* list box.
5. Click OK.

9 Click the Paste Options button and then click the Merge Formatting button (middle button) at the Paste Options button drop-down list.

10 Click the Word button on the taskbar and then click the **FCTThaiStats.docx** thumbnail.

11 Select the text *Resources:* and the three lines below it and then click the Copy button.

12 Click the Word button on the taskbar and then click the **3-FCTThailand.docx** thumbnail.

13 Move the insertion point to the end of the document and then press the Enter key.

14 Paste the copied text into the document without the formatting by clicking the Paste button arrow and then clicking *Paste Special* at the drop-down list.

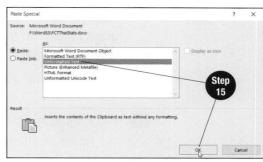

15 At the Paste Special dialog box, click *Unformatted Text* in the *As* list box and then click OK.

16 Select the four lines of text you just pasted in the document and then remove the spacing after the paragraphs by clicking the Layout tab and then clicking the *After* measurement box down arrow two times.

> Clicking the measurement down arrow two times will change the spacing after the selected paragraphs from 10 points to 0 points.

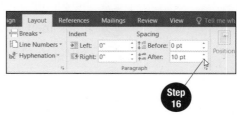

17 Save **3-FCTThailand.docx**.

18 Click the Word button on the taskbar, click the **FCTThaiStats.docx** thumbnail, and then close the document.

> Closing the **FCTThaiStats.docx** document displays the **3-FCTThailand.docx** document.

Check Your Work — Compare your work to the model answer to ensure that you have completed the activity correctly.

In Addition

Moving and Copying Text with the Mouse

You can move selected text using the mouse. To do this, select the text with the mouse and then move the I-beam pointer inside the selected text until the I-beam pointer turns into an arrow pointer. Click and hold down the left mouse button, drag the arrow pointer (displays with a gray box attached) to the location where you want to insert the selected text, and then release the button. Copy and move selected text by following similar steps, but hold down the Ctrl key while dragging with the mouse. When you hold down the Ctrl key, a box containing a plus symbol displays near the gray box by the arrow pointer.

Using the Clipboard task pane, you can collect up to 24 different items and then paste them in various locations in a document. Display the Clipboard task pane by clicking the Clipboard group task pane launcher. Cut or copy an item and the item displays in the Clipboard task pane. If the item is text, the first 50 characters display. Paste an item by positioning the insertion point at the desired location and then clicking the item in the Clipboard task pane. Once all desired items have been inserted, click the Clear All button in the upper right corner of the task pane.

What You Will Do You will open another document with information on Thailand, copy items in the document, and then paste the items into the Thailand document.

Tutorial
Using the Clipboard Task Pane

1 Make sure **3-FCTThailand.docx** is open and then open **FCTThaiInfo.docx**.

2 In **FCTThaiInfo.docx**, display the Clipboard task pane by clicking the Clipboard group task pane launcher [⌐]. If any items display in the Clipboard task pane, click the Clear All button in the upper right corner of the task pane.

Step 2

3 Select the *Food and Beverages* heading and the paragraph of text below it.

4 Click the Copy button in the Clipboard group.

Notice how the copied item is represented in the Clipboard task pane.

5 Select the *Shopping* heading and the paragraph of text below it.

6 Click the Copy button in the Clipboard group.

7 Select the *Entertainment* heading and the paragraph of text below it.

8 Click the Copy button in the Clipboard group.

9 Click the Word button on the taskbar and then click the *3-FCTThailand.docx* thumbnail.

10 Display the Clipboard task pane by clicking the Home tab and then clicking the Clipboard group task pane launcher.

11 Move the insertion point to the beginning of the *Accommodations* heading.

12 Click the item representing *Entertainment* in the Clipboard task pane.

Step 12

Use Clipboard Task Pane
1. Click Clipboard group task pane launcher.
2. Select text.
3. Click Copy button.
4. Select and copy any additional items.
5. Position insertion point.
6. Click item in Clipboard task pane.
7. Paste any other items from Clipboard task pane.
8. Click Clear All button.

13 Move the insertion point to the beginning of the *Points of Interest* heading.

14 Click the item representing *Shopping* in the Clipboard task pane.

15 Click the Clear All button in the upper right corner of the Clipboard task pane.

16 Close the Clipboard task pane by clicking the Close button ☒ in the upper right corner of the task pane.

17 Click the Word button on the taskbar, click the ***FCTThaiInfo.docx*** thumbnail, and then close the document.

> The **3-FCTThailand.docx** file displays when you close **FCTThaiInfo.docx**.

18 Press Ctrl + Home to move the insertion point to the beginning of the document.

19 Click anywhere in the title *THAILAND* and then click the *Title* style in the styles gallery on the Home tab.

20 Apply the Heading 1 style to the headings in the document (*Transportation, Traveling in Thailand, Attractions, Entertainment, Accommodations, Shopping, Points of Interest*, and *Passports/Visas*).

21 Click the Design tab and then click the *Casual* style set in the Document Formatting group.

22 Press Ctrl + Home to move the insertion point to the beginning of the document.

23 Center the title *THAILAND*.

24 Save **3-FCTThailand.docx**.

> **Check Your Work**   Compare your work to the model answer to ensure that you have completed the activity correctly.

In Addition

Using Clipboard Task Pane Options

Click the Options button at the bottom of the Clipboard task pane and a pop-up menu displays with five options as shown at the right. Insert a check mark before the options you want active. For example, you can choose to display the Clipboard task pane automatically when you cut or copy text, display the Clipboard task pane by pressing Ctrl + C twice, cut and copy text without displaying the Clipboard task pane, display the Office Clipboard icon on the taskbar when the Clipboard is active, or display a status message when copying items to the Clipboard. If the last option is selected, a message such as 2 of 24 - Clipboard displays at the right side of the taskbar.

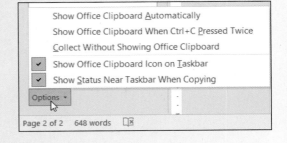

Activity 3.3 Customizing the Page Setup

In Word, a page contains default formatting such as a page size of 8.5 inches by 11 inches; top, bottom, left, and right margins of one inch; portrait page orientation; and a page break after approximately 9 inches of content on a page. You can change these defaults with buttons in the Page Setup group on the Layout tab. Change the default margins in a document with the Margins button. With the Orientation button, you can change the orientation from the default of portrait to landscape. Use the Size button in the Page Setup group to specify a paper size.

What You Will Do   To customize the Thailand document, you will change the document margins, orientation, and page size and apply a theme.

Tutorial
Changing Margins

Tutorial
Changing Page Orientation

Tutorial
Changing Paper Size

1 With **3-FCTThailand.docx** open, change the margins by clicking the Layout tab, clicking the Margins button in the Page Setup group, and then clicking the *Wide* option at the drop-down list.

> The *Wide* option changes the left and right margins to 2 inches each.

2 Change the page orientation by clicking the Orientation button in the Page Setup group on the Layout tab and then clicking *Landscape* at the drop-down list.

> Word considers a page in portrait orientation to be 8.5 inches wide and 11 inches tall. Word considers a page in landscape orientation to be 11 inches wide and 8.5 inches tall. You can also change page orientation at the Page Setup dialog box with the Margins tab selected.

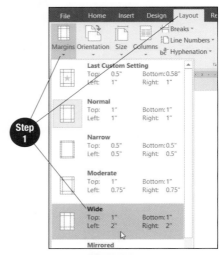

3 Change the margins again by clicking the Margins button in the Page Setup group on the Layout tab and then clicking the *Custom Margins* option at the bottom of the drop-down list.

4 At the Page Setup dialog box with the Margins tab selected and *2"* selected in the *Top* measurement box, type 0.8.

5 Click the *Bottom* measurement box down arrow until *0.8"* displays.

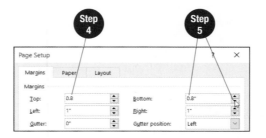

6 Click OK to close the Page Setup dialog box.

7 Change the paper size by clicking the Size button in the Page Setup group and then clicking the *Legal* option at the drop-down list.

8 Scroll through the document to view the pages in legal paper size.

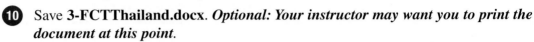

9 Change back to letter paper size by clicking the Size button and then clicking the *Letter* option at the drop-down list.

10 Save **3-FCTThailand.docx**. *Optional: Your instructor may want you to print the document at this point*.

11 Change the page orientation by clicking the Orientation button in the Page Setup group and then clicking *Portrait* at the drop-down list.

12 Change the margins by clicking the Margins button in the Page Setup group and then clicking *Normal* at the drop-down list.

13 Apply a theme to the document by clicking the Design tab, clicking the Themes button in the Document Formatting group, and then clicking *Integral* at the drop-down gallery.

14 Change the theme colors by clicking the Colors button in the Document Formatting group and then clicking *Red Orange* at the drop-down gallery.

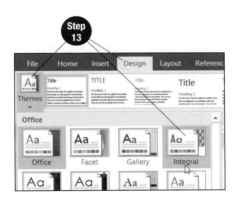
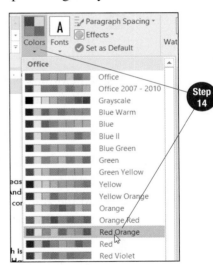

15 Save **3-FCTThailand.docx**.

Check Your Work — Compare your work to the model answer to ensure that you have completed the activity correctly.

In Addition

Applying Landscape Orientation

Can you imagine some instances in which you might use a landscape orientation? Suppose you are preparing a company's annual report and you need to include a couple of tables that have several columns of text. If you use the default portrait orientation, the columns will need to be quite narrow, possibly so narrow that reading becomes difficult. Changing the orientation to landscape results in three more inches of usable space. If you choose to use landscape orientation on one page, you are not committed to using it for the entire document. You can use portrait and landscape in the same document. To do this, select the text, display the Page Setup dialog box, click the desired orientation, and then change the *Apply to* option to *Selected text*.

The Page Background group on the Design tab contains buttons for inserting a watermark, changing the page background color, and inserting a page border. A watermark is lightened text or an image that displays behind text. Word provides a number of predesigned watermark images you can insert in a document. Apply a page background color using the Page Color button. Page background color appears on the screen but does not print. The Page Borders button in the Page Background group provides another method for displaying the Borders and Shading dialog box with the Page Border tab selected.

FIRST CHOICE
TRAVEL

What You Will Do   To make sure others know that the Thailand document is still in progress, you will insert a watermark. To add visual appeal to the document, you will apply page background color and a page border.

Tutorial
Inserting and
Removing a
Watermark

Tutorial
Applying Page
Background Color

1 With **3-FCTThailand.docx** open, press Ctrl + Home.

2 Insert a watermark by clicking the Design tab and then clicking the Watermark button 🗒 in the Page Background group.

3 Scroll down the Watermark button drop-down list and then click the *DRAFT 1* option.

4 Apply a page background color to the document by clicking the Page Color button 🗒 in the Page Background group.

5 Click the *Gold, Accent 5, Lighter 80%* color option (ninth column, second row).

> Page background color is designed for viewing a document on screen and does not print.

6 Click the Page Borders button in the Page Background group.

7 At the Borders and Shading dialog box with the Page Border tab selected, click the *Art* option box arrow.

8 Scroll down the list of page borders and then click the art border option shown below.

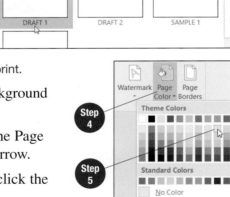

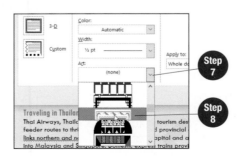

In Brief

Apply Watermark
1. Click Design tab.
2. Click Watermark button.
3. Click watermark option.

Apply Page Background Color
1. Click Design tab.
2. Click Page Color button.
3. Click color.

Apply Page Border
1. Click Design tab.
2. Click Page Borders button.
3. Click options at Borders and Shading dialog box.
4. Click OK.

9 Click OK to close the dialog box.

10 Save **3-FCTThailand.docx**.

11 Print **3-FCTThailand.docx**.

12 Remove the page border by clicking the Design tab and then clicking the Page Borders button.

13 At the Borders and Shading dialog box, click *None* in the *Setting* section.

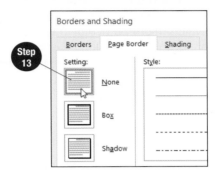

14 Click OK to close the dialog box.

15 Remove page background color by clicking the Page Color button in the Page Background group and then clicking *No Color*.

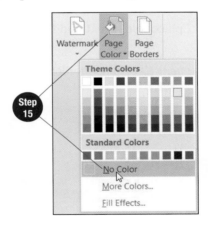

16 Save **3-FCTThailand.docx**.

Check Your Work Compare your work to the model answer to ensure that you have completed the activity correctly.

In Addition

Changing Page Border Options

By default, a page border displays and prints 24 points from the top, left, right, and bottom edges of the page. Some printers, particularly inkjet printers, have a non-printing area around the outside edges of the page that can interfere with the printing of a border. If part of a page border does not print, consider changing measurements at the Border and Shading Options dialog box. Display this dialog box by clicking the Design tab and then clicking the Page Borders button. At the Borders and Shading dialog box with the Page Border tab selected, click the Options button. At the dialog box, increase the margin measurements to move the page border away from the edges of the page and decrease the measurements to move the page border closer to the edges of the page.

Inserting a Cover Page, Blank Page, and Page Break

The Pages group on the Insert tab contains buttons for adding a cover page, a blank page, and a page break. Click the Cover Page button and a drop-down list displays with prede- signed cover pages. A cover page might include placeholders, which are locations where specific text is inserted. Insert a page break in a document with the keyboard shortcut Ctrl + Enter or with the Page Break button on the Insert tab. Use the Blank Page button to insert a blank page, which might be useful in a document where you want to insert a blank page for an illustration, graphic, or figure.

FIRST CHOICE
TRAVEL

What You Will Do   You will insert the Motion cover page in the Thailand document and insert specific text in the cover page placeholders. You will also insert a page break and a blank page in the document.

Tutorial
Inserting and Removing a Cover Page

Tutorial
Inserting and Removing a Blank Page

Tutorial
Inserting and Removing a Page Break

1. With **3-FCTThailand.docx** open, press Ctrl + Home.

2. Click the Insert tab and then click the Cover Page button 🔲 in the Pages group.

3. Insert a predesigned cover page by scrolling down the drop-down list and then clicking the *Motion* cover page option.

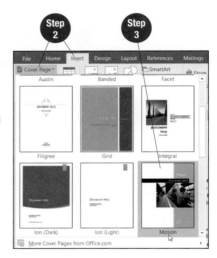

4. Click the *[Year]* placeholder text and then type the current year.

5. Click the *[Document title]* placeholder text and then type Discover Thailand.

6. Click the *[Company name]* placeholder text and then type First Choice Travel. If a company name already displays above the date in the bottom right corner, click the company name, click the Company tab, and then type First Choice Travel.

7. Select the name that displays above *First Choice Travel* and then type your first and last names.

8. Insert the current date below *First Choice Travel* by clicking the date, clicking the arrow at the right of the placeholder, and then clicking *Today*.

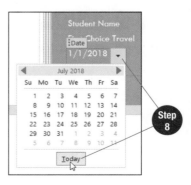

9. You need a blank page at the end of the document for information that will be added later. Press Ctrl + End to move the insertion point to the end of the document.

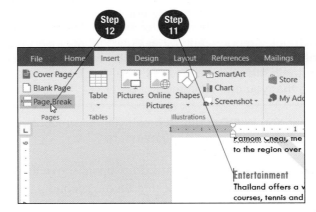

10 Click the Blank Page button in the Pages group.

11 Move the insertion point to the beginning of the heading *Entertainment*.

12 Insert a page break by clicking the Page Break button in the Pages group.

> You can also insert a hard page break with the keyboard shortcut Ctrl + Enter.

13 Save **3-FCTThailand.docx** and then print only pages 1 and 2.

14 Delete the page break you inserted in Step 12 by positioning the insertion point at the end of the paragraph of text below the *Attractions* heading and then pressing the Delete key two times.

15 Remove the blank page. Begin by clicking the Home tab and then clicking the Show/Hide ¶ button in the Paragraph group.

> Clicking the Show/Hide ¶ button on the Home tab turns on the displays of nonprinting characters such as a paragraph symbol to indicate the press of the Enter key and a small dot to indicate the press of the spacebar.

16 Position the insertion point at the beginning of the page break that displays on the third page and then press the Delete key two times.

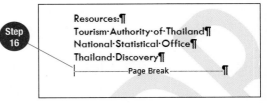

17 Click the Show/Hide ¶ button to turn off the display of nonprinting characters.

18 Save **3-FCTThailand.docx**.

Check Your Work — Compare your work to the model answer to ensure that you have completed the activity correctly.

In Addition

Inserting Page Breaks

Word assumes that you are using standard-sized paper, which is 8.5 inches wide and 11 inches long. With default top and bottom margins of 1 inch, a Word document can contain approximately 9 inches of content per page. At approximately the 10-inch mark, Word automatically inserts a page break. A page break inserted by Word is considered a *soft page break* and a page break you insert with the Page Break button or the keyboard shortcut, Ctrl + Enter, is considered a *hard page break*. A soft page break adjusts automatically as text is added or deleted from a document. A hard page break does not adjust and therefore will remain in the place you originally inserted it.

Insert page numbers in a document with the Page Number button or in a header or footer. Click the Page Number button in the Header & Footer group on the Insert tab and a drop-down list displays with options for inserting page numbers at the top or bottom of the page or in the page margins, removing page numbers, and formatting page numbers. Text that appears at the top of every page is called a *header* and text that appears at the bottom of every page is referred to as a *footer*. Headers and footers are common in manuscripts, textbooks, reports, and other publications. Insert a predesigned header in a document with the Header button in the Header & Footer group on the Insert tab. Insert a predesigned footer in the same manner as a header. Predesigned headers and footers contain formatting that you can customize.

What You Will Do Insert identifying information in the Thailand document using a header and footer and insert page numbers.

Tutorial
Inserting and Removing Page Numbers

Tutorial
Inserting and Removing a Predesigned Header and Footer

Tutorial
Editing a Header and Footer

1. With **3-FCTThailand.docx** open, move the insertion point to the beginning of the title *THAILAND* (located on the second page).

2. Click the Insert tab.

3. Insert page numbers at the bottom of each page by clicking the Page Number button in the Header & Footer group and then pointing to *Bottom of Page*.

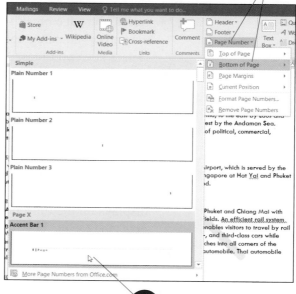

4. At the gallery of predesigned page numbers, click the *Accent Bar 1* option.

   The page number is inserted in the footer pane. With the footer pane active, the document is dimmed.

5. Click the Close Header and Footer button to close the footer pane and make the document active.

6. Scroll through the document and notice how the page numbers display toward the bottom of every page except the cover page.

7. Remove page numbering by clicking the Insert tab, clicking the Page Number button in the Header & Footer group, and then clicking *Remove Page Numbers* at the drop-down list.

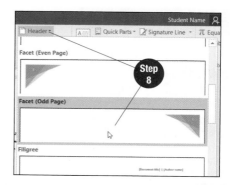

8. Insert a header in the document by clicking the Header button in the Header & Footer group, scrolling down the drop-down list, and then clicking the *Facet (Odd Page)* header.

9 Click the Close Header and Footer button to close the header pane and make the document active.

10 Click the Insert tab.

11 Insert a footer by clicking the Footer button in the Header & Footer group.

12 Scroll down the Footer button drop-down list and then click the *Ion (Dark)* footer.

> Notice how the document title you entered in the cover page is inserted in the footer, as is the author's name.

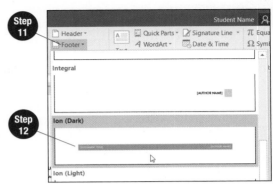

13 Click the Close Header and Footer button to close the footer pane and make the document active.

14 Scroll through the document and notice how the header and footer appear on each page except the cover page.

15 Remove the header by clicking the Insert tab, clicking the Header button in the Header & Footer group, and then clicking *Remove Header* at the drop-down list.

16 Insert a new header by clicking the Header button in the Header & Footer group, scrolling down the drop-down list, and then clicking the *Ion (Dark)* header.

17 Double-click in the body of the document.

> Close a header or footer pane by clicking the Close Header and Footer button or by double-clicking in the document.

18 Edit the footer by clicking the Insert tab, clicking the Footer button in the Header & Footer group, and then clicking *Edit Footer* at the drop-down list.

19 Press Ctrl + A to select the footer.

20 Change the font size by clicking the Home tab, clicking the *Font Size* option box arrow, and then clicking *10* at the drop-down list.

21 Click the Bold button to apply bold formatting.

22 Double-click in the document to close the footer pane and make the document active.

23 Save, print, and then close **3-FCTThailand.docx**.

Check Your Work ▸ Compare your work to the model answer to ensure that you have completed the activity correctly.

In Addition

Creating Your Own Header or Footer

Create your own header or footer using the *Edit Header* or *Edit Footer* options from the corresponding button drop-down list. For example, to create a header, click the Insert tab, click the Header button, and then click *Edit Header* at the drop-down list. This opens the header pane and also displays the Header & Footer Tools Design tab with buttons and options for editing the header. Make the desired edits to the header with options on the tab and then close the header pane by clicking the Close Header and Footer button in the Close group on the Header & Footer Tools Design tab. Complete similar steps to create your own footer.

When preparing a research paper or report, consider inserting sources, citations, and a bibliography or works cited page to give credit to the sources of words, ideas, and any material summarized or quoted. Word includes some common reference styles for citing and referencing research papers and reports, including the Modern Language Association (MLA) style, which is generally used in the humanities. To create a source, display the Create Source dialog box by clicking the References tab, clicking the Insert Citation button in the Citations & Bibliography group, and then clicking *Add New Source*. At the dialog box, insert bibliography information in the required fields. Once you insert source information in the Create Source dialog box, Word will automatically save the source information. To insert a citation in a document from a source that is already saved, click the Insert Citation button in the Citations & Bibliography group and then click the desired reference at the drop-down list. If you include a direct quote from a source, you will need to include the page number. To do this, click the citation in the document to select the citation placeholder, click the Citation Options arrow, and then click *Edit Citation* at the drop-down list. At the Edit Citation dialog box, type in the page or page numbers of the quote's source.

What You Will Do   You are responsible for preparing and formatting a report on Middleton Valley for First Choice Travel. You have been asked to format the report in the MLA style.

Tutorial
Formatting a Report in MLA Style

Tutorial
Inserting Sources and Citations

1 Open **FCTMiddletonRpt.docx** and then save it with the name **3-FCTMiddletonRpt**.

2 Click the References tab, click the *Style* option box arrow in the Citations & Biblography group, and then click *MLA* at the drop-down list.

> Refer to Table 3.1 for general guidelines on formatting a research paper or report in MLA style.

3 Press Ctrl + A to select the entire document and then change the font to 12-point Cambria.

4 With the text still selected, change the line spacing to double line spacing by clicking the Line and Paragraph Spacing button in the Paragraph group on the Home tab and then clicking *2.0* at the drop-down list.

5 With the text still selected, remove spacing after paragraphs by clicking the Layout tab, clicking in the *After* measurement box in the *Spacing* section, typing 0, and then pressing the Enter key.

Table 3.1 MLA Style General Guidelines

Use standard-sized paper (8.5 × 11 inches).
Set 1-inch top, bottom, left, and right margins.
Set text in a 12-point serif typeface (such as Cambria or Times New Roman).
Double-space text.
Indent the first line of each paragraph one-half inch.
Insert a header that prints in the upper right corner of each page the last name of the person writing the report followed by the page number.

6 Press Ctrl + Home to position the insertion point at the beginning of the document.

7 Type your name and then press the Enter key.

8 Type your instructor's name and then press the Enter key.

9 Type the title of your course and then press the Enter key.

10 Type the current date.

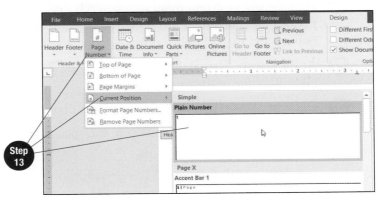

11 Insert a header in the document by clicking the Insert tab, clicking the Header button in the Header & Footer group, and then clicking *Edit Header* at the drop-down list.

12 Press the Tab key two times to move the insertion point to the right margin in the header pane, type your last name, and then press the spacebar.

13 Insert page numbers by clicking the Page Number button in the Header & Footer group on the Header & Footer Tools Design tab, pointing to *Current Position*, and then clicking the *Plain Number* option.

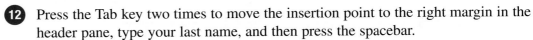
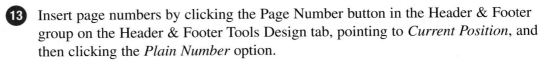

14 Press Ctrl + A to select the header and then change the font to 12-point Cambria.

15 Click the Close Header and Footer button.

16 Insert a new source in the document. Begin by positioning the insertion point immediately right of the word *constructed* (but before the period) that ends the fifth sentence in the second paragraph.

17 Click the References tab.

18 Click the Insert Citation button in the Citations & Bibliography group and then click *Add New Source* at the drop-down list.

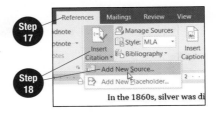

19 At the Create Source dialog box, click the *Type of Source* option box arrow and then click *Journal Article* at the drop-down list.

20 Click in the *Author* text box, type Joanne Henderson, and then press the Tab key three times.

21 Type Natural Resources of Middleton Valley in the *Title* text box and then press the Tab key.

22 Type Planet Earth's Resources in the *Journal Name* text box and then press the Tab key.

23 Type 2018 in the *Year* text box and then press the Tab key.

24 Type 7-9 in the *Pages* text box.

25 Click OK to close the Create Source dialog box.

26 Position the insertion point immediately right of the word *century* (but before the period) that ends the third sentence in the third paragraph, click the Insert Citation button, and then click *Add New Source* at the drop-down list.

27 At the Create Source dialog box, click the *Type of Source* option box arrow and then click *Web site* at the drop-down list.

28 Click the *Show All Bibliography Fields* check box to insert a check mark.

29 Type the following information in the specified fields:

> *Author* = Daniel Marcello
> *Name of Web Page* = Middleton Regional Planning Department
> *Year* = 2018
> *Month* = January
> *Day* = 5
> *Year Accessed* = (type current year)
> *Month Accessed* = (type current month)
> *Day Accessed* = (type current day)
> *URL* = emcp.org/middleton

30 After entering the information, click OK.

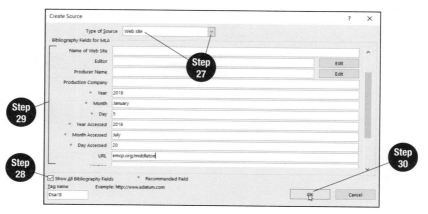

In Brief

Choose Reference Style
1. Click References tab.
2. Click *Style* option box arrow.
3. Click reference style.

Insert New Source
1. Click References tab.
2. Click Insert Citation button.
3. Click *Add New Source* option.
4. At Create Source dialog box, specify type of source.
5. Enter information in appropriate text boxes.
6. Click OK.

Insert Citation
1. Position insertion point in document.
2. Click References tab.
3. Click Insert Citation button.
4. Click reference.

Edit Citation
1. Click Citation Options arrow.
2. Click *Edit Citation* option.
3. Make changes at Edit Citation dialog box.
4. Click OK.

31 Insert a citation from an existing source. Begin by positioning the insertion point between the quotation mark after the word *erosion* and the period in the second sentence in the fourth paragraph.

32 Click the Insert Citation button in the Citations & Bibliography group and then click the *Henderson, Joanne* reference at the drop-down list.

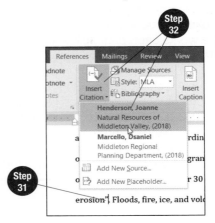

33 Because you are citing a direct quote, you need to include the page number of the journal article where you found the quote. Begin by clicking anywhere in the Henderson citation you just inserted.

This displays the citation placeholder.

34 Click the Citation Options arrow at the right side of the citation placeholder and then click *Edit Citation* at the drop-down list.

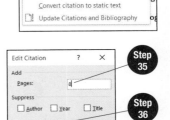

35 At the Edit Citation dialog box, type 8 in the *Pages* text box.

36 Click OK to close the Edit Citation dialog box.

37 Save **3-FCTMiddletonRpt.docx**.

Check Your Work — Compare your work to the model answer to ensure that you have completed the activity correctly.

In Addition

Formatting the First Page of an MLA-Formatted Report

Your instructor may require you to omit the header on the first page of the document. To remove the header from the first page of a document, press Ctrl + Home to move the insertion point to the beginning of the document, click the Header button in the Header & Footer group on the Insert tab, and then click *Edit Header* at the drop-down list. Click the *Different First Page* check box in the Options group on the Header & Footer Tools Design tab. This inserts a new header pane named *First Page Header*. Since you do not want a header on the first page, leave this header blank. Click the Next button in the Navigation group on the Header & Footer Tools Design tab and, if you previously created a header in the document, it displays in the header pane. If the document did not include a header, type or insert the desired header text in the header pane.

Once you include citations in a report or research paper, you need to insert a works cited page on a separate page at the end of the document. A works cited page is an alphabetic list of the books, journal articles, web pages, and any other sources referenced in the document. To insert a works cited page, click the References tab and then click the Bibliography button in the Citations & Bibliography group. At the Bibliography drop-down list, click the desired format option. After inserting sources into a document, you may need to edit a citation to correct errors or change data. One method for editing a source is to click the desired citation in the document, click the Citation Options arrow, and then click *Edit Source* at the drop-down list. This displays the Edit Source dialog box with the information you originally typed. Make desired changes and then click OK to close the dialog box. If you edit a source, Word will not automatically update the works cited. To update the works cited, click anywhere in the works cited page and then click the Update Citations and Bibliography tab.

What You Will Do To finish the Middleton Valley report, you need to add a works cited page, edit one of the sources, and apply MLA style formatting to the works cited page.

Tutorial

Inserting a Works
Cited Page

Tutorial

Editing a Citation
and Source

① With **3-FCTMiddletonRpt.docx** open, insert a works cited page at the end of the document. Begin by pressing Ctrl + End to move the insertion point to the end of the document and then pressing Ctrl + Enter to insert a hard page break.

② Click the References tab and then click the Bibliography button in the Citations & Bibliography group.

③ Click the *Works Cited* option in the *Built-In* section of the drop-down list.

④ You realize that part of the web page title is missing and you need to edit the source. Begin by clicking anywhere in the *Marcello* citation, located in the first paragraph on the second page.

This selects the citation placeholder.

⑤ Click the Citation Options arrow at the right side of the citation placeholder and then click *Edit Source* at the drop-down list.

This displays the Edit Source dialog box, which contains the same options as the Create Source dialog box.

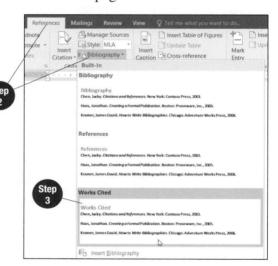

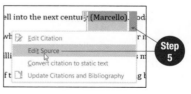

⑥ At the Edit Source dialog box, click in the *Name of Web Page* text box, edit the text so it displays as *Middleton Valley Regional Planning Department*, and then click OK to close the dialog box.

⑦ At the message telling you that the source exists in your master list and the current document and asking you if you want to update both, click Yes.

8 Update the works cited to include the edited source. Begin by pressing Ctrl + End to move the insertion point to the end of the document and then click anywhere in the works cited text.

9 Click the Update Citations and Bibliography placeholder tab.

> The placeholder tab displays above the *Works Cited* title. Notice that the updated works cited page includes the edited web page name.

10 Format the works cited page to MLA standards, which are listed in Table 3.2. Begin by selecting the *Works Cited* heading and the entries below it and then click the *No Spacing* style in the Styles group on the Home tab.

11 With the text still selected, change the font to Cambria, the font size to 12 points, and the line spacing to double line spacing.

12 Click anywhere in the title *Works Cited* and then click the Center button in the Paragraph group.

13 Hang-indent the works cited entries. Do this by selecting only the entries and then pressing Ctrl + T.

> You can also hang-indent the entries by clicking the Paragraph group dialog box launcher, clicking the *Special* list box arrow in the *Indentation* section, clicking *Hanging* at the drop-down list, and then clicking OK to close the Paragraph dialog box.

14 Press Ctrl + Home to move the insertion point to the beginning of the document.

15 Save, print, and then close **3-FCTMiddletonRpt.docx**.

Table 3.2 MLA Style Works Cited Page Formatting Guidelines

Begin works cited on a separate page at the end of the document.
Include the title *Works Cited* centered at the top of the page.
Double-space between and within entries.
Begin each entry at the left margin and hang-indent the second and subsequent lines in each entry.
Alphabetize the entries.

Check Your Work Compare your work to the model answer to ensure that you have completed the activity correctly.

In Addition

Modifying Sources at the Source Manager Dialog Box

Copy, delete, edit, and create new sources at the Source Manager dialog box. Display this dialog box by clicking the References tab and then clicking the Manage Sources button in the Citations & Bibliography group. The *Master List* section of the dialog box displays all of the citations you have created in Word, and the *Current List* section displays all of the citations included in the currently open document.

You can change paragraph alignment with the Click and Type feature. To use the Click and Type feature, position the mouse pointer at the left margin, in the center of the page, or at the right margin until the pointer displays with the desired alignment symbol and then double-click the mouse button. By default, text is aligned at the top of the page. Change this vertical alignment to center, justified, or bottom with the *Vertical alignment* option at the Page Setup dialog box with the Layout tab selected. Insert an image in a document from a location on the computer with the Pictures button on the Insert tab. Use the Online Pictures button on the Insert tab to search for images on the Internet. Format an inserted image with buttons and options on the Picture Tools Format tab. This tab is active when an image is selected.

What You Will Do   First Choice Travel is planning a workshop for people interested in traveling on a budget. You will create an announcement that contains center- and right-aligned text, vertically center the text on the page, and then add visual appeal by inserting an image and the company logo.

Tutorial
Using Click and Type

Tutorial
Vertically Aligning Data

Tutorial
Inserting, Sizing, and Positioning an Image

Tutorial
Formatting an Image

1   Press Ctrl + N to display a blank document and then press the Enter key.

2   Position the I-beam pointer in the document between the left and right margins at about the 3.25-inch mark on the horizontal ruler and approximately one inch from the top of the page. When the center alignment lines display below the I-beam pointer, double-click the left mouse button.

3   Type the centered text shown in Figure 3.1, pressing the Enter key between each line of text and twice after the last line of centered text.

4   Change to right alignment by positioning the I-beam pointer near the right margin at approximately the 6.5-inch mark on the horizontal ruler and the 2-inch mark on the vertical ruler. When the right alignment lines display at the left side of the I-beam pointer, double-click the left mouse button.

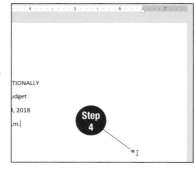

Figure 3.1 Step 3 and Step 5

TRAVELING INTERNATIONALLY

Traveling on a Budget

Thursday, April 19, 2018

7:00 to 8:30 p.m.

Sponsored by
First Choice Travel

5 Type the right-aligned text shown in Figure 3.1. After typing the first line of right-aligned text, press Shift + Enter to move the insertion point to the next line.

6 Select the centered text and then change the font to 14-point Candara bold. Select the right-aligned text, change the font to 10-point Candara bold, and then deselect the text.

7 Vertically center the text on the page. To do this, click the Layout tab and then click the Page Setup group dialog box launcher.

8 At the Page Setup dialog box, click the Layout tab, click the *Vertical alignment* option box arrow, and then click *Center* at the drop-down list.

9 Click OK to close the Page Setup dialog box.

10 Save the document and name it **3-FCTTravelIntl**.

11 Print **3-FCTTravelIntl.docx**.

12 Return the vertical alignment to top alignment. To do this, click the Page Setup group dialog box launcher. At the Page Setup dialog box, click the Layout tab, click the *Vertical alignment* option box arrow, and then click *Top* at the drop-down list. Click OK to close the dialog box.

13 Click the Insert tab and then click the Online Pictures button in the Illustrations group.

This displays the Insert Pictures window with a search text box.

14 At the Insert Pictures window, click in the search box, type travel suitcase globe, and then press the Enter key.

15 Double-click the image shown at the right. If this image is not available online, click the Pictures button on the Insert tab. At the Insert Picture dialog box, navigate to the folder containing your data documents and then double-click **Suitcases.png**.

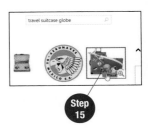

The image is inserted in the document, it is selected (sizing handles display around the image), and the Picture Tools Format tab displays as shown in Figure 3.2. A Layout Options button displays at the right side of the image. Click this button to display a list of options for positioning the image and wrapping text around the image.

Figure 3.2 Picture Tools Format Tab

16 With the image selected, click the Position button in the Arrange group and then click the *Position in Top Left with Square Text Wrapping* option (first column, first row in the *With Text Wrapping* section).

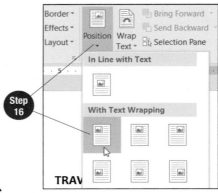

> Apply a text wrapping style to an image to specify how you want text or other items to flow around the image. Apply text wrapping with options from the Position button or with the Wrap Text button.

17 Add a shadow effect to the image by clicking the *Drop Shadow Rectangle* option in the Picture Styles group (fourth option).

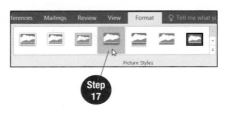

18 Click the Corrections button in the Adjust group and then click the *Brightness: 0% (Normal) Contrast: +40%* option (third column, bottom row in the *Brightness/Contrast* section).

19 Click the Picture Effects button in the Pictures Styles group, point to *Glow*, and then click the *Blue, 5 pt glow, Accent color 1* option (first column, first row in the *Glow Variations* section).

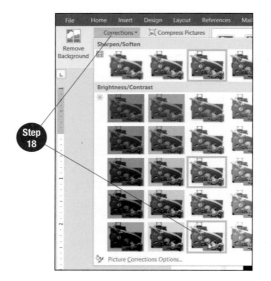

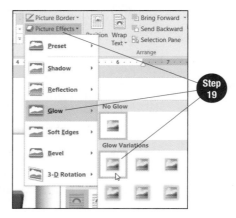

20 Click in the *Shape Height* measurement box in the Size group, type 1.7, and then press the Enter key.

> When you change the height measurement, the width measurement is automatically changed to maintain the proportions of the image.

21 Select and then delete the text *First Choice Travel* that displays in small font size at the right side of the document.

22 Insert the First Choice Travel logo image below *Sponsored by*. To begin, click the Insert tab and then click the Pictures button in the Illustrations group.

23 At the Insert Picture dialog box, navigate to the folder containing your data documents and then double-click *FCTLogo.jpg*.

In Brief

Vertically Center Text
1. Click Layout tab.
2. Click Page Setup group dialog box launcher.
3. Click Layout tab.
4. Click *Vertical alignment* option.
5. Click *Center*.
6. Click OK.

Insert Online Image
1. Click Insert tab.
2. Click Online Pictures button.
3. Type search text in search box and then press Enter.
4. Double-click image.

Insert Image from Computer
1. Click Insert tab.
2. Click Pictures button.
3. Navigate to folder.
4. Double-click image.

24 With the logo image selected in the document, click the Layout Options button 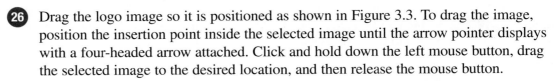 that displays outside the upper right corner of the image and then click *Tight* (second column, first row in *With Text Wrapping* section).

Step 24

25 With the logo image still selected, hold down the Shift key, click one of the corner sizing handles (white squares) and hold down the left mouse button; drag to reduce the size of the image so it displays as shown in Figure 3.3; and then release the mouse button.

> Holding down the Shift key while increasing or decreasing the size of an image maintains the proportions of the image.

26 Drag the logo image so it is positioned as shown in Figure 3.3. To drag the image, position the insertion point inside the selected image until the arrow pointer displays with a four-headed arrow attached. Click and hold down the left mouse button, drag the selected image to the desired location, and then release the mouse button.

> As you move an image near the top, left, right, or bottom margins of the document, green guidelines appear to help you position the image.

27 Click outside the logo to deselect it.

28 Save, print, and then close **3-FCTTravelIntl.docx**.

Figure 3.3 Activity 3.9

Check Your Work — Compare your work to the model answer to ensure that you have completed the activity correctly.

In Addition

Formatting an Image with Buttons on the Picture Tools Format Tab

Images inserted in a document can be formatted in a variety of ways, which might include adding fill color and border lines, increasing or decreasing the brightness or contrast, choosing a wrapping style, and cropping the image. Format an image with buttons on the Picture Tools Format tab as shown in Figure 3.2. With buttons in the Adjust group, you can correct the brightness and contrast of the image; change the image color; change to a different image; reset the image to its original size, position, and color; and compress the picture. Compress a picture to reduce resolution or discard extra information to save room on the hard drive or reduce download time. Use buttons in the Picture Styles group to apply a predesigned style, insert a picture border, or apply a picture effect. The Arrange group contains buttons for positioning the image, wrapping text around the image, and aligning and rotating the image. Use options in the Size group to crop the image and specify the height and width of the image.

Word automates the creation of envelopes with options at the Envelopes and Labels dialog box with the Envelopes tab selected. At this dialog box, type a delivery address and a return address. If you open the Envelopes and Labels dialog box in a document containing a name and address, the name and address are inserted automatically as the delivery address. If you enter a return address, Word will ask you before printing if you want to save the new return address as the default return address. Click the Yes button if you want to use the return address for future envelopes, or click the No button if you will use a different return address for future envelopes.

What You Will Do   You need to create an envelope for sending the information about Thailand to Camille Matsui at Marquee Productions.

Preparing an Envelope

1 Press Ctrl + N to display a blank document.

> You can also display a blank document by clicking the File tab, clicking the *New* option, and then clicking the *Blank document* template. Another method is to insert a New button on the Quick Access Toolbar and then click the button to display a blank document. To insert the New button on the Quick Access Toolbar, click the Customize Quick Access Toolbar button at the right side of the toolbar and then click *New* at the drop-down list.

2 Click the Mailings tab and then click the Envelopes button ▭ in the Create group.

3 At the Envelopes and Labels dialog box with the Envelopes tab selected, type the following name and address in the *Delivery address* text box. Press the Enter key at the end of each line, except the last line containing the city, state, and zip code.

> Camille Matsui
> Marquee Productions
> 955 South Alameda Street
> Los Angeles, CA 90037

④ If any text displays in the *Return address* text box, delete it and then type the following name and address. Type your name where you see *Student Name*.

First Choice Travel
Student Name
3588 Ventura Boulevard
Los Angeles, CA 90102

⑤ Click the Add to Document button.

Clicking the Add to Document button inserts the envelope in the document. You can also send the envelope directly to the printer by clicking the Print button.

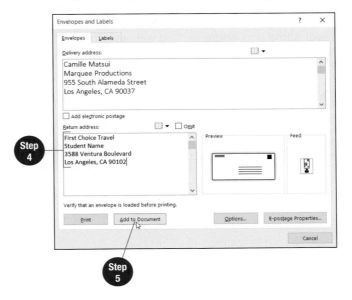

⑥ At the message asking if you want to save the new return address as the default address, click No.

⑦ Save the document with the name **3-FCTEnvtoMP**.

⑧ Print and then close **3-FCTEnvtoMP.docx**. *Note: Manual feed of the envelope may be required. Please check with your instructor before printing the envelope.*

Check Your Work Compare your work to the model answer to ensure that you have completed the activity correctly.

In Addition

Customizing Envelopes

With options at the Envelope Options dialog box shown at the right, you can customize an envelope. Display this dialog box by clicking the Options button at the Envelopes and Labels dialog box. At the Envelope Options dialog box, you can change the envelope size, change the font for the delivery and return addresses, and specify the positioning of the addresses in relation to the left and top edges of the envelope.

Activity 3.11 Preparing Mailing Labels

Use Word's Labels feature to print text on mailing labels, file labels, disc labels, or other types of labels. You can create labels for printing on a variety of predefined labels, which you can purchase at an office supply store. With the Labels feature, you can create a sheet of mailing labels with the same name and address or image or enter a different name and address on each label. Create a label with options at the Envelopes and Labels dialog box with the Labels tab selected.

What You Will Do   You will create a sheet of mailing labels containing the First Choice Travel name and address. You will also create mailing labels for sending the Thailand document to several First Choice Travel customers and create labels for the First Choice Travel office in Toronto.

Tutorial
Creating Mailing Labels with the Same Name and Address and an Image

Tutorial
Creating Mailing Labels with Different Names and Addresses

1 Press Ctrl + N to display a blank document.

2 Click the Mailings tab and then click the Labels button in the Create group.

3 Type the following information in the *Address* text box. Type your name where you see *Student Name*. (Press the Enter key at the end of each line except the last line.)

> First Choice Travel
> Student Name
> 3588 Ventura Boulevard
> Los Angeles, CA 90102

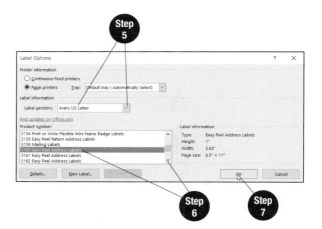

4 Click the Options button.

5 At the Label Options dialog box, click the *Label vendors* option box arrow and then click *Avery US Letter* at the drop-down list.

6 Scroll down the *Product number* list box and then click *5160 Easy Peel Address Labels*.

7 Click OK to close the dialog box.

8 Click the New Document button at the Envelopes and Labels dialog box.

9 Save the document and name it **3-FCTLALabels**.

10 Print and then close **3-FCTLALabels.docx**.

11 Click the Mailings tab and then click the Labels button in the Create group.

12 At the Envelopes and Labels dialog box, click the New Document button.

13 At the document, type the first name and address shown in Figure 3.4 in the first label. Press the Tab key two times to move the insertion point to the next label and then type the second name and address shown in Figure 3.4. Press the Tab key two times and then type the third name and address. Press the Tab key one time and then type the fourth name and address. Continue in this manner until you have typed all of the names and addresses in Figure 3.4.

Create Mailing Labels with Same Name and Address
1. Click Mailings tab.
2. Click Labels button.
3. Type name and address in *Address* text box.
4. Click either New Document button or Print button.

Create Mailing Labels with Different Names and Addresses
1. Click Mailings tab.
2. Click Labels button.
3. Click New Document button.
4. At document screen, type names and addresses.

Create Mailing Labels with Image
1. Click Insert tab.
2. Click Pictures button.
3. Navigate to folder.
4. Double-click image.
5. Click Mailings tab.
6. Click Labels button.
7. Click New Document button.

⑭ Save the document and name it **3-FCTCustLabels**.

⑮ Print and then close **3-FCTCustLabels.docx**.

⑯ At the blank document, create mailing labels for the Toronto office of First Choice Travel using an image. Begin by clicking the Insert tab and then clicking the Pictures button in the Illustrations group.

⑰ At the Insert Picture dialog box, navigate to the folder containing your data files and then double-click *FCTTorontoLabel.jpg*.

⑱ With the label image selected, click the Position button in the Arrange group on the Picture Tools Format tab and then click the *Position in Top Center with Square Text Wrapping* option (second column, first row in the *With Text Wrapping* section).

⑲ With the image still selected, click the Mailings tab and then click the Labels button.

⑳ At the Envelopes and Labels dialog box, make sure the Avery US Letter label number 5160 is selected and then click the New Document button.

> When you click the New Document button, the label image is inserted in each label in the page and inserted in a new document.

㉑ Save the document and name it **3-FCTTorontoLabels**.

㉒ Print and then close **3-FCTTorontoLabels.docx**.

㉓ Close the document containing the label image without saving it.

Figure 3.4 Step 13

Moreno Products 350 Mission Boulevard Pomona, CA 91767	Mr. Miguel Santos 12120 Barranca Parkway Irvine, CA 92612	Mr. and Mrs. Jack Lipinski 5534 Eagle Ridge Drive Los Angeles, CA 90092
Dr. Esther Riggins 9077 Walnut Street Los Angeles, CA 90097	Automated Services, Inc. 4394 Seventh Street Long Beach, CA 92602	Ms. Samantha Schwartz 103-B Pacific Palms Los Angeles, CA 90068

Check Your Work — Compare your work to the model answer to ensure that you have completed the activity correctly.

In Addition

Customizing Labels

Click the Options button at the Envelopes and Labels dialog box with the Labels tab selected and the Label Options dialog box displays as shown at the right. At this dialog box, choose the type of printer, the desired label vendor, and the product number. This dialog box also displays information about the selected label, such as type, height, width, and paper size. When you select a label, Word automatically determines label margins. If, however, you want to customize these default settings, click the Details button at the Label Options dialog box.

Features Summary

Feature	Ribbon Tab, Group	Button, Option	Keyboard Shortcut
blank page	Insert, Pages		
Clipboard task pane	Home, Clipboard		
copy selected text	Home, Clipboard		Ctrl + C
cover page	Insert, Pages		
Create Source dialog box	References, Citations & Bibliography	, *Add New Source*	
cut selected text	Home, Clipboard		Ctrl + X
Envelopes and Labels dialog box with Envelopes tab selected	Mailings, Create		
Envelopes and Labels dialog box with Labels tab selected	Mailings, Create		
footer	Insert, Header & Footer		
hanging indent			Ctrl + T
header	Insert, Header & Footer		
Insert Picture dialog box	Insert, Illustrations		
Insert Pictures window	Insert, Illustrations		
page background color	Design, Page Background		
page borders	Design, Page Background		
page break	Insert, Pages		Ctrl + Enter
page margins	Layout, Page Setup		
page number	Insert, Header & Footer		
page orientation	Layout, Page Setup		
Page Setup dialog box	Layout, Page Setup		
paper size	Layout, Page Setup		
paste selected text	Home, Clipboard		Ctrl + V
Paste Special dialog box	Home, Clipboard	, *Paste Special*	
watermark	Design, Page Background		
works cited page	References, Citations & Bibliography		

Workbook Section study tools and assessment activities are available in the *Workbook* ebook. These resources are designed to help you further develop and demonstrate mastery of the skills learned in this section.

Formatting with Special Features

Data Files ▶ Before beginning section work, copy the WordS2 folder to your storage medium and then make WordS2 the active folder.

Skills

- Create and modify WordArt text
- Create a drop cap
- Insert a text box and draw a text box
- Insert and modify shapes
- Use SmartArt to create organizational charts and diagrams
- Create, format, and modify tables
- Insert one file into another

- Insert a continuous section break
- Format text into columns and modify columns
- Insert a hyperlink
- Save a document in PDF format
- Merge letters and envelopes
- Edit a data source file

Precheck ▶ Check your current skills to help focus your study of the skills taught in this section.

Projects Overview

 Format a document on special vacation activities in Hawaii; prepare an organizational chart and graphic of services; create and modify a table containing information on scenic flights on Maui; format and modify a fact sheet containing information on Petersburg, Alaska; save the fact sheet as a single file web page and insert hyperlinks to an additional document and a website; create a data source file and then merge a letter on cruise specials and an envelope document with the data source file; format a newsletter containing information on Zenith Adventures.

 Create an organizational chart and graphic for the production department.

 **NIAGARA PENINSULA COLLEGE** Create and format a table with information on classes offered by the Theatre Arts Division; format and modify a newsletter.

 Create a data source file and then merge it with a letter asking for fabric pricing; create an organizational chart and graphic for the design department.

 Create and format a table containing information on catered lunch options; create a flyer.

 Create and format an announcement about an upcoming stockholders' meeting.

 SNAP If you are a SNAP user, launch the Precheck and Tutorials from your Assignments page.

Model Answers ▶ Preview the model answers for an overview of the projects you will complete in the section activities.

Activity 4.1 Creating and Modifying WordArt Text

Use the WordArt feature to distort or modify text to conform to a variety of shapes. Consider using WordArt to create a company logo, letterhead, flyer title, or heading. To insert WordArt, click the Insert tab, click the WordArt button in the Text group, and then click the desired WordArt style at the drop-down gallery. When WordArt is selected, the Drawing Tools Format tab displays. Use options and buttons on this tab to modify and customize WordArt.

What You Will Do To increase the visual appeal of a document on Hawaiian specials, you decide to insert and format WordArt.

Tutorial
Inserting, Sizing, and Positioning WordArt

Tutorial
Formatting WordArt

1 Open **FCTHawaiianSpecials.docx** and then save it with the name **4-FCTHawaiianSpecials**.

2 Complete a spelling and grammar check on the document. You determine what to correct and what to ignore. (The name *Molokini* is spelled correctly in the document.)

3 Click the Design tab, click the Fonts button in the Document Formatting group, scroll down the drop-down gallery, and then click *Calibri Light-Constantia*.

4 Click the Colors button and then click the *Green* option at the drop-down gallery.

5 With the insertion point positioned at the beginning of the document, click the Insert tab.

6 Insert WordArt by clicking the WordArt button [A] in the Text group and then clicking the *Gradient Fill - Aqua, Accent 1, Reflection* option (second column, second row).

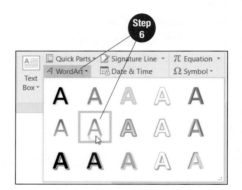

Step 6

7 Type HAWAIIAN SPECIALS.

> This inserts the WordArt text *HAWAIIAN SPECIALS* in the document, selects the WordArt text box, and displays the Drawing Tools Format tab.

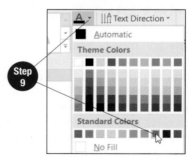

Step 9

8 Select the border of the WordArt by positioning the arrow pointer on the dashed border that surrounds the WordArt and then clicking the left mouse button. (This changes the dashed border to a solid line border.)

9 Click the Text Fill button arrow [A▾] in the WordArt Styles group and then click the *Blue* option (eighth option in the *Standard Colors* section).

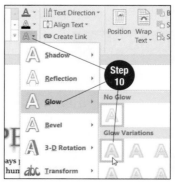

Step 10

10 Click the Text Effects button [A▾] in the WordArt Styles group, point to *Glow*, and then click the *Green, 5 pt glow, Accent color 1* option (first column, first row in the *Glow Variations* section).

11 Increase the height of the WordArt text box by clicking in the *Shape Height* measurement box in the Size group, typing 1, and then pressing the Enter key.

12 Increase the width of the WordArt text box by clicking in the *Shape Width* measurement box in the Size group, typing 6.5, and then pressing the Enter key.

13 Click the Position button in the Arrange group and then click the *In Line with Text* option (first option in the drop-down gallery).

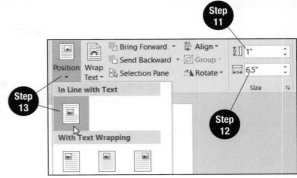

14 Click the Text Effects button in the WordArt Styles group, point to *Transform*, and then click the *Deflate* option (second column, sixth row in the *Warp* section).

15 Apply the Heading 2 style to the following headings: *White Sands Charters*, *Air Adventures*, *Deep Sea Submarines*, *Snorkeling Fantasies*, and *Bicycle Safari*.

16 Press Ctrl + A to select the entire document, click the Home tab, click the Font Color button arrow, and then click the *Turquoise, Accent 6, Darker 50%* option (last column, last row in the *Theme Colors* section).

17 Save **4-FCTHawaiianSpecials.docx**.

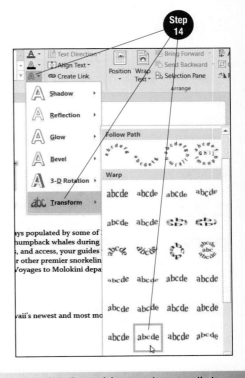

Check Your Work Compare your work to the model answer to ensure that you have completed the activity correctly.

In Addition

Using the Drawing Tools Format Tab

When WordArt is selected, the Drawing Tools Format tab displays as shown below. Use options in the Insert Shapes group to draw a shape or text box. With options in the Shape Styles group, you can apply a predesigned style, change the shape fill color and the shape outline color, and apply shape effects. Change the style of the WordArt text with options in the WordArt Styles group, apply text formatting to WordArt with options in the Text group, specify the layering of the WordArt text with options in the Arrange group, and identify the height and width of the WordArt text box with measurement boxes in the Size group.

Use a drop cap to enhance the appearance of text. A drop cap is the first letter of the first word of a paragraph that is set into a paragraph. Drop caps identify the beginning of major sections or parts of a document. Create a drop cap with the Drop Cap button in the Text group on the Insert tab. Use the Text Box button in the Text group to create a text box or insert a predesigned text box in a document. The Shapes button in the Illustrations group on the Insert tab contains a number of shape options for drawing shapes in a document including lines, rectangles, basic shapes, block arrows, flow chart shapes, stars, banners, and callouts. Click a shape and the mouse pointer displays as crosshairs. Position the crosshairs where you want the shape positioned and then click the left mouse button or click and hold down the left mouse button, drag to create the shape, and then release the mouse button. This inserts the shape in the document and also displays the Drawing Tools Format tab. Use buttons on this tab to change the shape, apply a style to the shape, arrange the shape, and change the size of the shape.

What You Will Do You will continue to add visual appeal to the Hawaiian Specials document by creating a drop cap and a shape and inserting a predesigned text box.

Tutorial
Creating and Removing a Drop Cap

Tutorial
Inserting a Text Box

Tutorial
Formatting a Text Box

Tutorial
Inserting, Sizing, and Positioning a Shape and Line

Tutorial
Formatting a Shape and Line

1 With **4-FCTHawaiianSpecials.docx** open, position the insertion point anywhere in the heading *White Sands Charters*, click the Border button arrow in the Paragraph group on the Home tab, and then click *Borders and Shading* at the drop-down list.

2 At the Borders and Shading dialog box, make sure the single line is selected in the *Style* list box, click the *Color* option box arrow, and then click the *Turquoise, Accent 6, Darker 50%* option (last column, last row in the *Theme Colors* section).

3 Click the bottom of the diagram in the *Preview* section of the dialog box.

> This inserts a single turquoise line in the diagram.

4 Click OK to close the Borders and Shading dialog box.

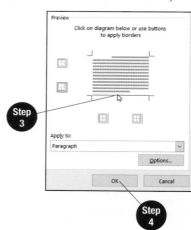

5 Use the Repeat command, F4, to apply the same turquoise bottom border to the remaining headings in the document (*Air Adventures*, *Deep Sea Submarines*, *Snorkeling Fantasies*, and *Bicycle Safari*).

6 Move the insertion point to the beginning of the word *Sail* that displays immediately below the heading *White Sands Charters* and then click the Insert tab.

7 Click the Drop Cap button in the Text group and then click *Dropped* at the drop-down gallery.

> If you click *Drop Cap Options*, the Drop Cap dialog box displays with options for positioning the drop cap, changing the font, identifying the number of lines for the drop cap, and setting the distance from the drop cap to the text.

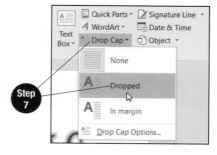

8 Click anywhere in the text on the first page to deselect the *S*.

9 Insert a text box on the first page by clicking the Text Box button 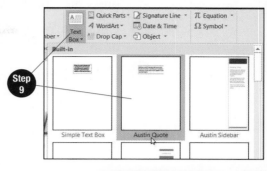 in the Text group on the Insert tab and then clicking the *Austin Quote* option.

> Predesigned text boxes are listed in alphabetical order.

10 Type the following text in the text box: Sign up today for your Hawaiian adventure and enjoy spectacular beaches, Hawaii's natural undersea world, and beautiful bays.

11 With the Drawing Tools Format tab active, click the More Shape Styles button 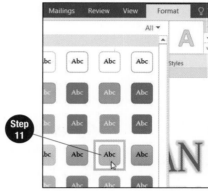 in the Shape Styles group and then click the *Subtle Effect - Aqua, Accent 5* option (sixth column, fourth row in the *Theme Styles* section).

12 Click the dashed line border of the text box to change the border to a solid line border.

> To apply formatting to the text in the text box, the border must be changed from a dashed line to a solid line.

13 Click the Text Fill button arrow and then click the *Turquoise, Accent 6, Darker 50%* option (last column, last row in the *Theme Colors* section).

14 With the text still selected, press Ctrl + B to apply bold formatting and then press Ctrl + Shift + < to decrease the font size.

15 Click the Shape Effects button, point to *Glow*, and then click the *Turquoise, 5 pt glow, Accent color 6* option (last column, first row in the *Glow Variations* section).

16 Click the Shape Effects button, point to *Bevel*, and then click the *Circle* option (first column, first row in the *Bevel* section).

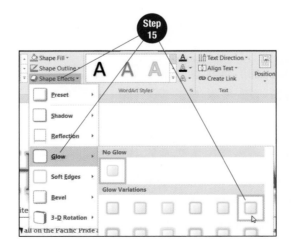

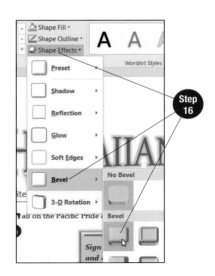

17 Click in the *Shape Width* measurement box in the Size group, type **2.9**, and then press the Enter key.

18 Click the Wrap Text button in the Arrange group and then click *Tight* at the drop-down gallery.

19 Drag the text box so it is positioned similarly to what is shown below.

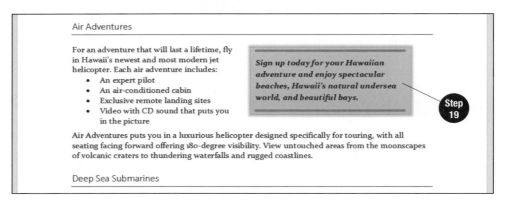

20 Press Ctrl + End to move the insertion point to the end of the document and then press the Enter key two times.

21 Click the Insert tab and then click the Shapes button in the Illustrations group.

22 Click the *Bevel* shape (first column, third row in the *Basic Shapes* section).

23 Click in the document at the location of the insertion point.

> This inserts a bevel shape in the document that is 1.14 inches in width and height.

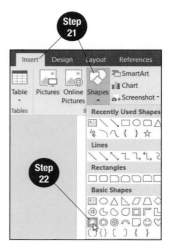

24 Apply a shape style by clicking the More Shape Styles button in the Shape Styles group and then clicking the *Subtle Effect - Aqua, Accent 5* option (sixth column, fourth row in the *Theme Styles* section).

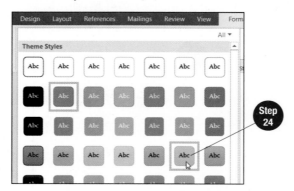

25 Click in the *Shape Height* measurement box, type 1.5, and then press the Enter key.

26 Click in the *Shape Width* measurement box, type 5.5, and then press the Enter key.

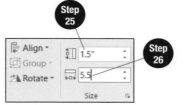

27 Click the Align button ⊞ in the Arrange group and then click *Distribute Horizontally* at the drop-down list.

28 With the shape selected, type Sign up today for your Hawaiian adventure!

29 Select the text you just typed.

> To format text in a text box or shape, you can click the border line to change it from a dashed line border to a solid line border, or select the text in the text box or shape.

30 Click the Home tab, change the font size to 14 points, change the font color to standard dark blue, and then apply bold and italic formatting.

> Your text box should appear similar to what is shown below.

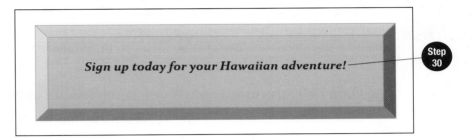

Sign up today for your Hawaiian adventure!

31 Press Ctrl + Home to move the insertion point to the beginning of the document.

32 Save, print, and then close **4-FCTHawaiianSpecials.docx**.

Check Your Work   Compare your work to the model answer to ensure that you have completed the activity correctly.

In Addition

Drawing Lines

The Shapes button drop-down list contains a number of options for drawing lines in a document. Click the *Curve* option in the *Lines* section to draw curved lines by clicking at the beginning position, dragging to the location where you want the curve to appear, and then clicking the mouse button again. Continue in this manner until you have drawn all the desired curved lines. Click the *Freeform* option in the *Lines* section to draw freeform in a document. After clicking the *Freeform* option, drag in the document screen. When you want to stop drawing, double-click the left mouse button. You can also use the *Scribble* option to draw freeform in a document. The difference between the Freeform tool and the Scribble tool is that you have to double-click to stop drawing with the Freeform tool but you only need to release the mouse button to stop drawing with the Scribble tool.

Drawing and Formatting Text Boxes

Draw your own text box in a document by clicking the Insert tab, clicking the Text Box button in the Text group, and then clicking *Draw Text Box* at the drop-down list. The mouse pointer displays as crosshairs. Position the crosshairs in the document and then drag to create the text box. When you insert a text box in a document, the Drawing Tools Format tab becomes active. Use options on this tab to customize and format the text box.

Use SmartArt to create a variety of graphics to visually illustrate and present data. SmartArt includes graphics for presenting hierarchical data; making lists of data; showing data processes, cycles, and relationships; and presenting data in a matrix or pyramid. To display SmartArt graphics, click the Insert tab and then click the SmartArt button in the Illustrations group. This displays the Choose a SmartArt Graphic dialog box with *All* selected in the left panel and all available predesigned graphics displayed in the middle panel. Click the desired graphic type in the left panel and then click a graphic in the middle panel and the name of the graphic displays in the right panel along with a description of the graphic type. Double-click a graphic in the middle panel and the graphic is inserted in the document. Use buttons on the SmartArt Tools Design tab and the SmartArt Tools Format tab to customize a graphic. Some graphics are designed to include text. Type text in a graphic by selecting the object and then typing text in the object or by typing text in the *Type your text here* window at the left side of the graphic.

What You Will Do　Terry Blessing, president of First Choice Travel, has asked you to prepare a document containing information on the organizational structure of the company and a graphic that illustrates the services provided by First Choice Travel.

Tutorial
Inserting, Sizing, and Positioning SmartArt

Tutorial
Formatting SmartArt

1 Open **FCTStructure.docx** and then save it with the name **4-FCTStructure**.

2 Move the insertion point a double space below the heading *ORGANIZATIONAL CHART* and then create the organizational chart SmartArt graphic shown in Figure 4.1. To begin, click the Insert tab and then click the SmartArt button in the Illustrations group.

3 At the Choose a SmartArt Graphic dialog box, click *Hierarchy* in the left panel and then double-click the first option in the middle panel, *Organization Chart*.

> This displays the organizational chart in the document with the SmartArt Tools Design tab selected. Use buttons on this tab to add additional boxes, change the order of the boxes, choose a different layout, apply formatting with a SmartArt Style, and reset the formatting of the organizational chart SmartArt graphic.

4 If a *Type your text here* window displays at the left side of the SmartArt graphic, close it by clicking the Text Pane button in the Create Graphic group.

> You can also close the window by clicking the Close button in the upper right corner of the window.

5 Delete the bottom right box in the graphic by clicking the border of the box to select it and then pressing the Delete key.

> Make sure that the selection border that surrounds the box is a solid line and not a dashed line. If a dashed line displays, click the box border again to change it to a solid line.

6 With the bottom right box selected, click the Add Shape button arrow in the Create Graphic group and then click *Add Shape Below*.

> Your organizational chart SmartArt graphic should contain the same boxes as shown in Figure 4.1.

7 Click the *[Text]* placeholder in the top box, type Terry Blessing, press the Enter key, and then type President. Click in each of the remaining boxes and type the text as shown in Figure 4.1.

8 Click inside the SmartArt graphic border but outside any objects in the graphic.

> This deselects the shape in the SmartArt graphic but keeps the graphic selected.

9 Click the More SmartArt Styles button in the SmartArt Styles group.

10 Click the *Inset* option (second column, first row in the *3-D* section).

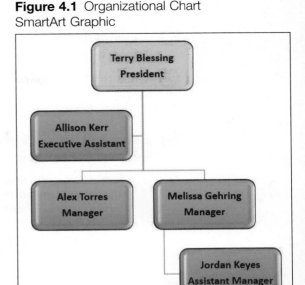

Figure 4.1 Organizational Chart SmartArt Graphic

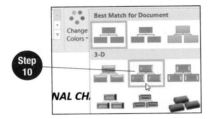

11 Click the Change Colors button in the SmartArt Styles group and then click the *Colorful Range - Accent Colors 5 to 6* option (last option in the *Colorful* section).

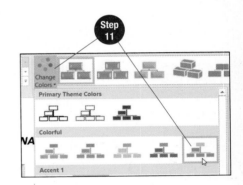

12 Click the SmartArt Tools Format tab.

> The SmartArt Tools Format tab contains buttons for changing the box shape; applying shape styles; applying WordArt styles to text; applying text fill, outline, and effects; and arranging and sizing the SmartArt graphic.

13 Click the tab (contains a left-pointing triangle) at the left side of the diagram border.

14 Click anywhere in the *Type your text here* window and then press Ctrl + A.

> This selects all of the text and shapes in the graphic.

15 Click the Change Shape button in the Shapes group and then click the *Rounded Rectangle* option (second shape in the *Rectangles* section).

16 Click the Shape Outline button arrow in the Shape Styles group and then click the *Dark Blue* color option (ninth option in the *Standard Colors* section).

17 Click the Text Fill button arrow in the WordArt Styles group and then click the *Dark Blue* color option in the *Standard Colors* section.

18 Press Ctrl + B to apply bold formatting to the text.

19 Close the Text pane by clicking the Close button in the upper right corner of the pane.

20 Deselect the shapes (but not the graphic) by clicking inside the SmartArt graphic border but outside any objects.

21 Click the Size button 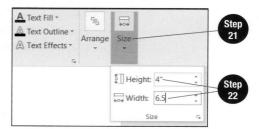 at the right side of the SmartArt Tools Format tab. (Your size options may display in the Size group rather than the Size button. If so, proceed to Step 22.)

22 Click in the *Shape Height* measurement box, type 4, click in the *Shape Width* measurement box, type 6.5, and then press the Enter key.

> In addition to the *Shape Height* and *Shape Width* measurement boxes, you can increase or decrease the size of a SmartArt graphic by dragging a corner of the graphic border. To maintain the proportions of the graphic, hold down the Shift key while dragging the border.

23 Press Ctrl + End to move the insertion point below the title *TRAVEL SERVICES* on the second page.

24 Click the Insert tab and then click the SmartArt button in the Illustrations group.

25 At the Choose a SmartArt Graphic dialog box, click *Cycle* in the left panel and then double-click the *Radial Cycle* graphic (second column, third row).

26 Click in each of the shapes in the graphic and then type the text as shown in Figure 4.2.

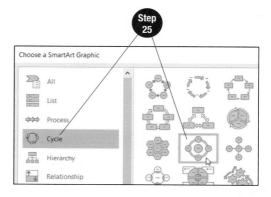

Figure 4.2 Services Diagram

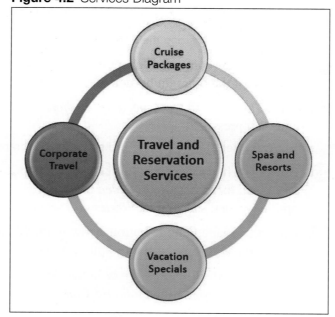

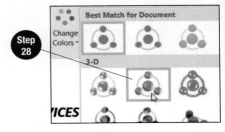

27 Click inside the graphic but outside any objects.

28 Click the More SmartArt Styles button in the SmartArt Styles group and then click the *Inset* option (second column, first row in the *3-D* section).

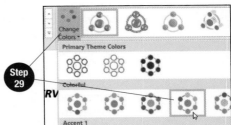

29 Click the Change Colors button in the SmartArt Styles group and then click the *Colorful Range - Accent Colors 4 to 5* option (fourth option in the *Colorful* section).

30 Click the SmartArt Tools Format tab.

31 Hold down the Shift key, click each of the circles in the graphic, and then release the Shift key.

> This selects all of the circle shapes in the graphic.

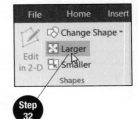

32 Click the Larger button 🔲 in the Shapes group to slightly increase the size of the circles.

33 Click the Shape Outline button arrow in the Shape Styles group and then click the *Dark Blue* color option (ninth option in the *Standard Colors* section).

34 Click the Text Fill button arrow in the WordArt Styles group and then click the *Dark Blue* color option in the *Standard Colors* section.

35 Press Ctrl + B to apply bold formatting to the text.

36 Deselect the circle shapes by clicking inside the graphic but outside any objects.

37 Click the Size button, click in the *Shape Height* measurement box, type 4, click in the *Shape Width* measurement box, type 6.5, and then press the Enter key. (Your size options may display in the Size group rather than the Size button.)

38 Click outside the graphic to deselect it.

39 Save, print, and then close **4-FCTStructure.docx**.

> **Check Your Work**   Compare your work to the model answer to ensure that you have completed the activity correctly.

In Addition

Moving or Positioning a SmartArt Graphic

Before moving a SmartArt graphic, apply text wrapping with options at the Position button drop-down gallery or the Wrap Text button drop-down gallery. With a text wrapping option applied, move a SmartArt graphic by positioning the arrow pointer on the graphic border until the pointer displays with a four-headed arrow attached, clicking and holding down the left mouse button, and then dragging the graphic to the desired location. As you move a graphic near the top, left, right, or bottom margins of the document, green guidelines appear to help you position the image.

Word's Table feature is useful for displaying data in columns and rows. This data may be text, values, and/or formulas. Create a table using the Table button on the Insert tab or with options at the Insert Table dialog box. Once you specify the desired number of rows and columns, Word displays the table and you are ready to enter information into the cells. A cell is the box created by the intersection of a column and a row. With the insertion point positioned in a table, two tabs are available for modifying and formatting the table—the Table Tools Design tab and the Table Tools Layout tab. Use options and buttons on the Table Tools Layout tab to perform such actions as selecting a table, row, or the entire table; inserting or deleting rows and/or columns; changing the height and width of rows and columns; and specifying text alignment in cells. You can also click the Properties button to display the Table Properties dialog box with options for vertically and horizontally centering a table on the page.

What You Will Do You are developing a new First Choice Travel information document about sightseeing flights around the island of Maui. You will create a table to display the data and then modify the table structure and apply formatting to the table and its cells.

Tutorial
Creating a Table

Tutorial
Changing the Table Layout

Tutorial
Customizing Cells in a Table

1. Open **FCTIslandFlights.docx** and then save it with the name **4-FCTIslandFlights**.

2. Press Ctrl + End to move the insertion point to the end of the document.

3. Click the Insert tab and then click the Table button in the Tables group.

4. Drag the mouse pointer down and to the right until the number above the grid displays as *3x6* and then click the mouse button.

5. Type the text in the cells as shown in Figure 4.3. Press the Tab key to move the insertion point to the next cell or press Shift + Tab to move the insertion point to the previous cell.

> When typing text in the cells in the second column, do not press the Enter key to end a line. Type the text and let the word wrap feature wrap the text within the cell. After typing text in the last cell, do not press the Tab key. This will insert another row. If you press the Tab key accidentally, immediately click the Undo button. To move the insertion point to different cells within the table using the mouse, click in the desired cell.

Figure 4.3 Step 5

Adventure	Destination	Price
Special West Maui	Waterfalls, lush tropical valleys	$49
West Maui Tropical	West Maui mountains, Hawaii's highest waterfalls	$79
Haleakala-Keane	Haleakala crater, tropical rain forest, waterfalls	$89
Special Circle Island	Hana, Haleakala, West Maui mountains, tropical rain forest, waterfalls	$169
Molokai-West Maui	West Maui mountains, waterfalls, sea cliffs, Kalaupapa colony	$189

6 You decide to add First Choice Travel discount prices to the table. To do this, position the insertion point in the *Price* cell, make sure the Table Tools Layout tab is active, and then click the Insert Right button ![Insert Right] in the Rows & Columns group.

Figure 4.4 shows the Table Tools Layout tab.

7 Click in the top cell of the new column, type FCT, and then press the Down Arrow key. Type the money amounts in the remaining cells as shown at the right. (Press the Down Arrow key to move to the next cell down.)

8 Delete the *Special Circle Island* row. To do this, click anywhere in the text *Special Circle Island*, make sure the Table Tools Layout tab is active, click the Delete button ![Delete] in the Rows & Columns group, and then click *Delete Rows* at the drop-down list.

9 Insert a row above *Adventure*. To do this, click anywhere in the text *Adventure* and then click the Insert Above button ![Insert Above] in the Rows & Columns group.

10 With the new top row selected, merge the cells by clicking the Merge Cells button ![Merge Cells] in the Merge group.

11 Type MAUI FLIGHTS in the top row.

12 Select all cells in the table by clicking the table move handle that displays in the upper left corner of the table (a square with a four-headed arrow inside).

13 Click the Home tab, change the font to Constantia and the font size to 12 points, and then click outside the table to deselect it.

14 Click in the top cell containing the text *MAUI FLIGHTS* and then click the Table Tools Layout tab.

15 Click in the *Table Row Height* measurement box in the Cell Size group, type 0.4, and then press the Enter key.

16 Insert a new column by clicking the Insert Left button ![Insert Left] in the Rows & Columns group.

17 With the cells in the new column selected, click the Merge Cells button in the Merge group.

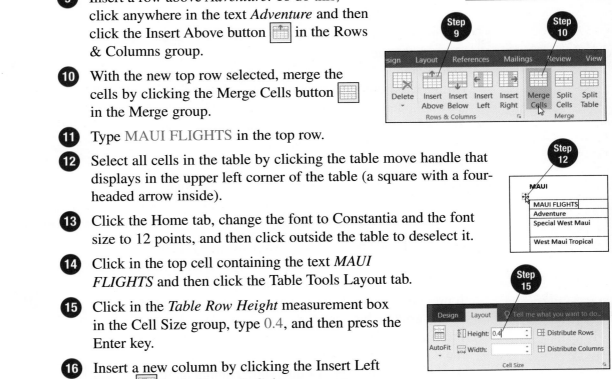

Figure 4.4 Table Tools Layout Tab

18 Type Hawaiian Adventures in the new cell.

19 Click two times on the Text Direction button  in the Alignment group.

20 Click the Align Center button in the Alignment group to change the horizontal and vertical alignment of text in the cell.

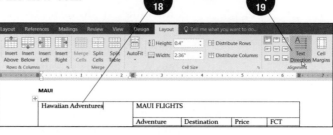

21 Position the mouse pointer on the gridline between the first and second columns until the pointer turns into a double-headed arrow pointing left and right with a short double line between. Click and hold down the left mouse button, drag to the left until the table column marker displays at approximately the 0.5-inch mark on the horizontal ruler, and then release the mouse button.

22 Position the mouse pointer on the gridline between the second and third columns until the pointer turns into a double-headed arrow pointing left and right with a short double line in between, click and hold down the left mouse button, drag to the left until the table column marker displays at the 2.25-inch mark on the horizontal ruler, and then release the mouse button.

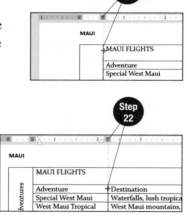

23 Following the same procedure, drag the gridline between the third and fourth columns to the left until the table column marker displays at the 4.25-inch mark on the horizontal ruler.

24 If you hold down the Alt key while dragging a gridline, column measurements display on the horizontal ruler. Use these measurements to change the width of the fourth column. To do this, position the mouse pointer on the gridline between the fourth and fifth columns, press and hold down the Alt key, click and hold down the left mouse button, drag the gridline to the left until the measurement for the fourth column on the horizontal ruler displays as *0.68"*, release the Alt key, and then release the mouse button.

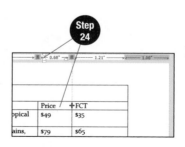

25 Position the mouse pointer on the gridline at the right side of the table, press and hold down the Alt key, click and hold down the left mouse button, drag the gridline to the left until the measurement for the fifth column on the horizontal ruler displays as *0.68"*, release the Alt key, and then release the mouse button.

26 Click anywhere in the *MAUI FLIGHTS* text and then click the Align Center button in the Alignment group on the Table Tools Layout tab.

This changes the horizontal and vertical alignment for text in the cell to center.

27 Select the four cells containing the headings *Adventure*, *Destination*, *Price*, and *FCT*. To do this, position the mouse pointer in the *Adventure* cell, click and hold down the left mouse button, drag to the *FCT* cell, and then release the mouse button.

28 With the cells selected, click the Align Center button in the Alignment group and then press Ctrl + B to apply bold formatting.

29 Select all of the cells containing prices and then click the Align Top Center button in the Alignment group.

30 Horizontally center the table on the page. Begin by clicking the Properties button in the Table group.

31 At the Table Properties dialog box with the Table tab selected, click the *Center* option in the *Alignment* section.

32 Click OK to close the Table Properties dialog box.

33 Click anywhere outside the table to deselect the cells.

34 Save **4-FCTIslandFlights.docx**.

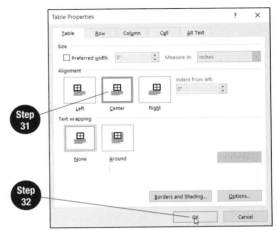

Check Your Work Compare your work to the model answer to ensure that you have completed the activity correctly.

In Addition

Creating a Table Using Other Methods

Other methods for creating a table include using options at the Insert Table dialog box or drawing a table. Display the Insert Table dialog box by clicking the Insert tab, clicking the Table button, and then clicking *Insert Table* at the drop-down list. Specify the desired number of columns and rows and then click OK to close the dialog box. Another method for creating a table is to draw a table by clicking the Table button and then clicking

Draw Table at the drop-down list. The mouse pointer changes to a pencil. Drag in the document screen to create the desired columns and rows.

Selecting Cells with the Keyboard

Besides using the mouse, you can also select cells using the following keyboard shortcuts:

To select	Press
the next cell's contents	Tab
the preceding cell's contents	Shift + Tab
the entire table	Alt + 5 (on the numeric keypad with Num Lock off)
adjacent cells	Hold Shift key and then press an arrow key repeatedly.
a column	Position insertion point in top cell of column, hold down Shift key, and then press Down Arrow key until column is selected.

Activity 4.5   Changing the Table Design

The Table Tools Design tab contains a number of options for enhancing the appearance of the table. With options in the Table Styles group, apply a predesigned style that applies color and border lines to a table. Maintain further control over the predesigned style formatting applied to columns and rows with options in the Table Style Options group. Apply additional formatting to cells in a table with the Shading button in the Tables Styles group and the Borders button in the Borders group. With options in the Borders group, you can customize the borders of cells in a table. Display a list of predesigned border lines; change the line style, width, and color; add or remove borders; and apply the same border style formatting to other cells with the Border Painter button.

What You Will Do   You will add final design formatting to the Maui Flights table by applying a table style and then customizing the formatting with additional options.

Tutorial
Changing the Table Design

Tutorial
Sorting Text in a Table

1　With **4-FCTIslandFlights.docx** open, select *MAUI FLIGHTS*, change the font size to 16 points, and apply bold formatting.

2　Select the text *Hawaiian Adventures*, change the font size to 14 points, and then apply bold and italic formatting.

3　Click anywhere in the table and then click the Table Tools Design tab.

4　Click the More Table Styles button in the Table Styles group.

>　This displays a drop-down gallery of style choices.

5　Click the *Grid Table 4 - Accent 2* option (third column, fourth row in the *Grid Tables* section; this location may vary, reference the image below to see how the option appears in the gallery).

>　Notice the color and border style formatting applied and also notice how the style changed the cell alignment for *MAUI FLIGHTS* and *Hawaiian Adventures* from Align Center to Align Top Center.

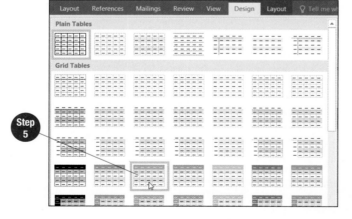

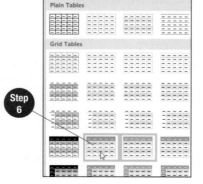

6　Experiment with an additional style by clicking the More Table Styles button and then clicking the *Grid Table 4 - Accent 1* option (second column, fourth row in the *Grid Tables* section).

7 Change the formatting by clicking the *Banded Rows* check box in the Table Style Options group to remove the check mark. Click the *Banded Columns* check box to insert a check mark. Click the *Header Row* check box to remove the check mark and click the *First Column* check box to remove the check mark.

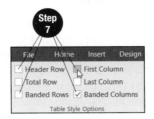

8 Save and then print **4-FCTIslandFlights.docx**.

9 With the insertion point positioned in a cell in the table and the Table Tools Design tab selected, click the *Header Row* check box in the Table Style Options group to insert a check mark, and click the *First Column* check box to insert a check mark. Click the *Banded Columns* check box to remove the check mark, and click the *Banded Rows* check box to insert a check mark.

10 Applying the table styles removed the horizontal alignment of the table. Horizontally align the table by clicking the Table Tools Layout tab, clicking the Properties button in the Table group, clicking the *Center* option in the *Alignment* section of the Table Properties dialog box, and then clicking OK to close the dialog box.

11 Apply the Heading 1 style to the headings *ISLAND SIGHTSEEING FLIGHTS* and *MAUI*.

12 Click the Design tab and then apply the Lines (Simple) style set, change the theme colors to Blue Green, and change the theme fonts to Calibri Light-Constantia.

13 Save, print, and then close **4-FCTIslandFlights.docx**.

> **Check Your Work** Compare your work to the model answer to ensure that you have completed the activity correctly.

In Addition

Sorting in a Table

Sort text in a table alphabetically, numerically, or by date with options at the Sort dialog box. Display this dialog box by positioning the insertion point in a cell in the table and then clicking the Sort button in the Data group on the Table Tools Layout tab. Make sure the column you want to sort is selected in the *Sort by* option and then click OK. If the first row in the table contains data such as headings that you do not want to include in the sort, click the *Header row* option in the *My list has* section of the Sort dialog box. If you want to sort specific cells in a table, select the cells first and then click the Sort button.

Inserting a Row Using the Mouse

You can use the mouse to insert a row by moving the mouse pointer immediately left of the row where you want the new row inserted. As you move the mouse pointer to the left side of a row, a plus symbol inside a circle displays along with thin, blue, double lines across the top or bottom of the row. Move the symbol and lines to the bottom of the row and then click the plus symbol and a new row is inserted below the current row. Move the symbol and lines to the top of the row and then click the plus symbol and a row is inserted above the current row.

Use the Object button in the Text group on the Insert tab to insert one document into another. To increase the ease with which a person can read and understand groups of words (referred to as the *readability* of a document), consider setting text in a document in newspaper columns. Newspaper columns contain text that flows up and down on the page. Create newspaper columns with the Columns button in the Page Setup group on the Layout tab or with options at the Columns dialog box. If you want to apply column formatting to only a portion of a document, insert a section break in the document with options at the Breaks button drop-down list.

What You Will Do   You are working on an informational document on Petersburg, Alaska, and realize that you need to insert additional information from another file. You also decide to improve the readability of the document by formatting the text into newspaper columns.

Tutorial
Inserting a File

Tutorial
Inserting and Deleting a Section Break

Tutorial
Formatting Text into Columns

1 Open **FCTPetersburgAK.docx** and then save it with the name **4-FCTPetersburgAK**.

2 Press Ctrl + End to move the insertion point to the end of the document and then click the Insert tab.

3 Insert a document into the current document by clicking the Object button arrow in the Text group and then clicking *Text from File* at the drop-down list.

4 At the Insert File dialog box, navigate to the WordS4 folder on your storage medium and then double-click *FCTPetersburgActivities.docx*.

5 Select the text you just inserted and then change the font to Constantia.

6 Apply the Heading 1 style to the title *PETERSBURG, ALASKA* and apply the Heading 2 style to the headings in the document: *Services*, *Visitor Attractions*, *Walking Tours*, *Accommodations*, *Transportation*, and *Guided Activities*.

7 Position the insertion point at the beginning of the first paragraph in the document (the paragraph that begins *Petersburg, Alaska, located on*) and then click the Layout tab.

8 Click the Breaks button in the Page Setup group. At the Breaks button drop-down list, click *Continuous* in the *Section Breaks* section.

Click one of the other three options in the *Section Breaks* section of the Breaks button drop-down list if you want to insert a section break that begins a new page.

9 Click the View tab and then click the Draft button in the Views group.

The section break is not visible in Print Layout view. A continuous section break separates the document into sections but does not insert a page break. In Draft view, the section break displays in the document as a double row of dots with the words *Section Break (Continuous)* in the middle.

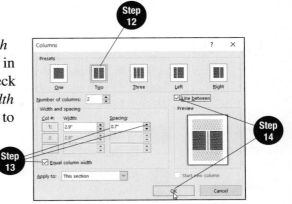

In Brief

Insert One File into Another
1. Click Insert tab.
2. Click Object button arrow.
3. Click *Text from File* option.
4. At Insert File dialog box, double-click document.

Insert Continuous Section Break
1. Click Layout tab.
2. Click Breaks button.
3. Click *Continuous*.

Format Text into Columns
1. Click Layout tab.
2. Click Columns button.
3. Click number of columns.

Display Columns Dialog Box
1. Click Layout tab.
2. Click Columns button.
3. Click *More Columns* option.

10 With the insertion point positioned below the section break, format the text below the section break into three newspaper columns by clicking the Layout tab, clicking the Columns button in the Page Setup group, and then clicking *Three* at the drop-down list.

> Formatting text into columns automatically changes the view to Print Layout.

11 As you view the document, you decide that the three columns are too narrow. To change the columns, click the Columns button in the Page Setup group and then click *More Columns* at the drop-down list.

12 At the Columns dialog box, click *Two* in the *Presets* section.

13 Increase the spacing between the two columns by clicking the *Spacing* measurement box up arrow in the *Width and spacing* section until *0.7"* displays in the measurement box. Make sure a check mark displays in the *Equal column width* check box. (If not, click the check box to insert the check mark.)

14 Click the *Line between* check box to insert a check mark and then click OK to close the dialog box.

> Inserting a check mark in the *Line between* check box inserts a line between the two columns. The *Preview* section of the dialog box shows you what this will look like.

15 Insert page numbering by clicking the Insert tab, clicking the Page Number button in the Header & Footer group, pointing to *Bottom of Page*, and then clicking the *Plain Number 2* option.

16 Click the Close Header and Footer button.

17 Press Ctrl + End to move the insertion point to the end of the document. Looking at the columns on the last (second) page, you decide to balance the two columns. To do this, click the Layout tab, click the Breaks button in the Page Setup group, and then click *Continuous* in the *Section Breaks* section.

18 Save and then print **4-FCTPetersburgAK.docx**.

Check Your Work | Compare your work to the model answer to ensure that you have completed the activity correctly.

In Addition

Changing Column Width

One method for changing column width in a document is to drag the column marker on the horizontal ruler. To change the width (and also the spacing) of columns of text, position the arrow pointer on the left or right edge of a column marker on the horizontal ruler until the pointer turns into a double-headed arrow pointing left and right.

Click and hold down the left mouse button, drag the column marker to the left or right to make the column wider or narrower, and then release the mouse button. Press and hold down the Alt key while dragging the column marker and measurements display on the horizontal ruler.

Insert a hyperlink in a document to navigate to a specific location in the document, display a different document, open a file in a different program, or link to an email address or web site. Insert a hyperlink with the Hyperlink button on the Insert tab. If a Word document is going to be distributed to others, consider saving the document in PDF format. The abbreviation *PDF* stands for *portable document format*, which is a file format that preserves fonts, formatting, and images in a printer-friendly version that looks the same on most computers. Someone who receives a Word file saved in PDF format does not need to have the Word application on his or her computer to open, read, and print the file. Exchanging PDF files is a popular method for collaborating with others. A Word document can be saved in PDF format through the Export backstage area or with the *Save as type* option at the Save As dialog box.

What You Will Do   A document with additional information on Petersburg, Alaska, is available and you decide to link that document to the current document by inserting a hyperlink. You also decide to insert a hyperlink to an Alaska travel website. Since some of First Choice Travel's clients do not have the Word application on their computers, you decide to save the Petersburg document in PDF format.

Tutorial
Inserting and Editing a Hyperlink

Tutorial
Saving and Opening a Document in PDF Format

1. With **4-FCTPetersburgAK.docx** open, press Ctrl + End to move the insertion point to the end of the document and then type Additional Information.

2. Select the text *Additional Information*.

3. Insert a hyperlink by clicking the Insert tab and then clicking the Hyperlink button 🌐 in the Links group.

4. At the Insert Hyperlink dialog box, click the *Look in* option box arrow, navigate to the WordS4 folder on your storage medium, and then double-click **FCTPetersburgStats.docx**.

   The Insert Hyperlink dialog box closes and *Additional Information* displays as hyperlinked text.

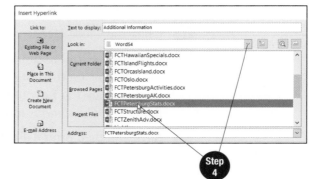

5. Press Ctrl + End, press the Enter key, and then type Alaska Tourism.

6. Create a hyperlink to the tourism site by selecting *Alaska Tourism* and then clicking the Hyperlink button in the Links group.

7. At the Insert Hyperlink dialog box, type www.travelalaska.com in the *Address* text box and then click OK.

   Word automatically adds *http://* to the beginning of the web address. If this website is not available, try www.state.ak.us.

In Brief

Insert Hyperlink
1. Select text.
2. Click Insert tab.
3. Click Hyperlink button.
4. Type file name or web address.
5. Click OK.

Save Document in PDF Format
1. Click File tab.
2. Click Export option.
3. Click Create PDF/XPS button.
4. Click Publish button.
5. Click Close button.

8 Display the document containing additional information on Petersburg by holding down the Ctrl key and then clicking the <u>Additional Information</u> hyperlink.

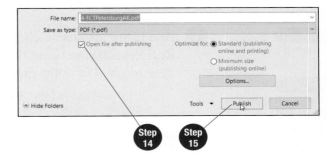

9 After reading the information in the document, close the document.

10 Make sure you are connected to the Internet and then connect to the Alaska tourism site by holding down the Ctrl key and then clicking the <u>Alaska Tourism</u> hyperlink.

> If you are not able to connect to the Alaska Tourism website, check with your instructor.

11 At the Alaska Tourism web site, click any hyperlinks that interest you. When you are finished, click the Close button in the upper right corner of the browser window.

12 Save a copy of the document as in PDF format. Begin by clicking the File tab and then clicking the *Export* option.

13 At the Export backstage area, click the Create PDF/XPS button.

14 At the Publish as PDF or XPS dialog box, make sure the WordS4 folder on your storage medium is the active folder and that the *Open file after publishing* check box contains a check mark.

15 Click the Publish button.

> This saves the document with the name **4-FCTPetersburgAK.pdf** and opens the document in Adobe Acrobat Reader.

16 After viewing the document in Adobe Acrobat Reader, click the Close button in the upper right corner of the window.

> Acrobat Acrobat Reader closes and the Word document displays on the screen.

17 Print only page 2 of the document.

18 Save and then close **4-FCTPetersburgAK.docx**.

Check Your Work   Compare your work to the model answer to ensure that you have completed the activity correctly.

In Addition

Downloading and Saving Web Pages and Images

You can save the image(s) and/or text that display when you open a web page as well as the web page itself. Copyright laws protect much of the information on the Internet, so check the site for restrictions before copying or downloading. If you do use information, make sure you properly cite the source. To save a web page as a file, display the desired page, right-click the page and then click *Save as* at the shortcut menu. At the Save

As dialog box, specify the folder where you want to save the web page. Select the text in the *File name* text box, type a name for the page, and then click the Save button. Save a specific web image by right-clicking the image and then clicking *Save image as*. At the Save As dialog box, type a name for the image in the *File name* text box and then press the Enter key.

If you need to mail the same basic letter to a number of clients or customers, consider using the Mail Merge feature to make the job easier and to make the letter more personalized. With Mail Merge, you can merge a data source file containing information on your clients with a main document containing the letter. You can also create an envelope document you can merge with a data source file. Click the Mailings tab to display a number of buttons for preparing a mail merge document. Generally, a merge takes two documents—the data source file and the main document. The data source file contains the variable information that will be inserted in the main document. Use buttons on the Mailings tab to create main documents and data source files for merging.

FIRST CHOICE TRAVEL

What You Will Do   First Choice Travel is offering a special cruise package, and Melissa Gehring has asked you to prepare a data source file with client information, merge it with a letter describing the cruise special, and then print envelopes for the letters.

Tutorial
Creating a Data Source File

Tutorial
Creating a Main Document

Tutorial
Previewing and Merging Documents

Tutorial
Merging Envelopes

1 At a blank document, click the Mailings tab, click the Select Recipients button 📇 in the Start Mail Merge group, and then click *Type a New List* at the drop-down list.

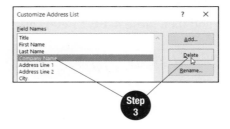

> This displays the New Address List dialog box with predesigned fields. You can use these predesigned fields as well as create your own custom fields.

2 Click the Customize Columns button at the bottom of the dialog box.

> The predesigned fields cover most of the fields you need for your data source file, but you decide to delete six of the predesigned fields and insert two of your own.

3 At the Customize Address List dialog box, click *Company Name* to select it and then click the Delete button.

4 At the message that displays, click Yes.

5 Complete steps similar to those in Steps 3 and 4 to delete the following fields: *Address Line 2*, *Country or Region*, *Home Phone*, *Work Phone*, and *E-mail Address*.

6 Click the Add button.

> If the New Address List dialog box does not provide for all variable information, create your own custom field.

7 At the Add Field dialog box, type Membership and then click OK.

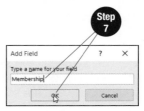

8 Click the Add button, type Discount, and then click OK.

9 Click OK to close the Customize Address List dialog box.

10 At the New Address List dialog box with the insertion point positioned in the *Title* field, type Mrs. and then press the Tab key.

> Pressing the Tab key moves the insertion point to the *First Name* field. Press the Tab key to move the insertion point to the next field and press Shift + Enter to move it to the previous field.

11 Continue typing text in the specified fields as indicated in Figure 4.5. After entering all of the information for the last client, click OK.

> After typing *3 percent* for Jerome Ellington, do not press the Tab key. If you do, a new blank client record will be created. To remove a blank record, click the Delete Entry button and then click Yes at the message.

12 At the Save Address List dialog box, navigate to your WordS4 folder. Click in the *File name* text box, type 4-FCTDataSource, and then press the Enter key.

> Word automatically saves the data source file as an Access database.

13 Open **FCTCruiseLtr.docx** and then save it with the name **4-FCTCruiseLtrMainDoc**.

14 Click the Mailings tab, click the Select Recipients button in the Start Mail Merge group, and then click *Use an Existing List* at the drop-down list.

Figure 4.5 Step 11

Title	Mrs.	*Title*	Mr. and Mrs.
First Name	Kristina	*First Name*	Walter
Last Name	Herron	*Last Name*	Noretto
Address Line 1	4320 Jackson Street	*Address Line 1*	3420 114th Avenue
City	Long Beach	*City*	Glendale
State	CA	*State*	CA
ZIP Code	90801	*ZIP Code*	91201
Membership	Premiere Choice	*Membership*	Ultimate Choice
Discount	3 percent	*Discount*	5 percent
Title	Ms.	*Title*	Mr.
First Name	Cathy	*First Name*	Jerome
Last Name	Washington	*Last Name*	Ellington
Address Line 1	321 Wildwood Street	*Address Line 1*	12883 22nd Street
City	Torrance	*City*	Inglewood
State	CA	*State*	CA
ZIP Code	90501	*ZIP Code*	90301
Membership	Ultimate Choice	*Membership*	Premiere Choice
Discount	5 percent	*Discount*	3 percent

15 At the Select Data Source dialog box, navigate to your WordS4 folder and then double-click *4-FCTDataSource.mdb*.

16 Move the insertion point a double space above the first paragraph of text in the letter and then click the Address Block button in the Write & Insert Fields group.

17 At the Insert Address Block dialog box, click OK.

> This inserts the necessary field code to insert the client name and address in the letter.

18 Press the Enter key two times and then click the Greeting Line button in the Write & Insert Fields group.

19 At the Insert Greeting Line dialog box, click the arrow at the right side of the option box containing the comma (the box to the right of the one containing *Mr. Randall*) and then click the colon at the drop-down list.

20 Click OK to close the dialog box.

21 Move the insertion point to the end of the first paragraph, type With your, and then press the spacebar.

22 Insert the *Membership* field by clicking the Insert Merge Field button arrow and then clicking *Membership* at the drop-down list.

23 Press the spacebar, type membership, you will receive an additional, and then press the spacebar.

24 Insert the *Discount* field by clicking the Insert Merge Field button arrow and then clicking *Discount* at the drop-down list.

25 Press the spacebar, type discount, and then type a period.

> The sentence you just typed should look like this: *With your «Membership» membership, you will receive an additional «Discount» discount.*

26 Click the Save button on the Quick Access Toolbar.

27 Merge the letter with the records in the data source file. Begin by clicking the Finish & Merge button in the Finish group on the Mailings tab and then clicking *Edit Individual Documents* at the drop-down list.

28 At the Merge to New Document dialog box, click OK.

> The letters are merged with the records and displayed in a new document.

29 Save the merged letters in the normal manner and name the document **4-FCTMergedCruiseLtrs**.

In Brief

Mail Merge
1. Click Mailings tab.
2. Click Select Recipients button.
3. Click *Type a New List*.
4. Click Customize Columns button.
5. At Customize Address List dialog box, delete and/or insert fields.
6. Click OK.
7. At New Address List dialog box, type text in fields.
8. Click OK.
9. At Save Address List dialog box, navigate to folder.
10. Click in *File name* text box, type name, press Enter.
11. Open main document.
12. Click Mailings tab.
13. Click Select Recipients button.
14. Click *Use an Existing List*.
15. At Select Data Source dialog box, navigate to folder, double-click data source file.
16. Insert fields in document.
17. Click Finish & Merge button.
18. Click OK.

30 Print and then close **4-FCTMergedCruiseLtrs.docx**.

Four letters will print.

31 Save and then close **4-FCTCruiseLtrMainDoc.docx**.

32 At a blank document, prepare envelopes for the four letters. Begin by clicking the Mailings tab, clicking the Start Mail Merge button, and then clicking *Envelopes* at the drop-down list.

33 At the Envelope Options dialog box, click OK.

34 Click the Select Recipients button in the Start Mail Merge group and then click *Use an Existing List* at the drop-down list.

35 At the Select Data Source dialog box, navigate to the WordS4 folder and then double-click **4-FCTDataSource.mdb**.

36 Click in the approximate location in the envelope in the document where the client's name and address will appear.

This causes a box with a dashed gray border to display. If you do not see this box, try clicking in a different location on the envelope.

37 Click the Address Block button in the Write & Insert Fields group.

38 At the Insert Address Block dialog box, click OK.

39 Click the Finish & Merge button in the Finish group and then click *Edit Individual Documents* at the drop-down list.

40 At the Merge to New Document dialog box, click OK.

41 Save the merged envelopes document and name it **4-FCTMergedEnvs**.

42 Print **4-FCTMergedEnvs.docx**.

This document will print four envelopes. Check with your instructor about specific steps for printing envelopes. You may need to hand feed envelopes into your printer.

43 Close **4-FCTMergedEnvs.docx**.

44 Close the envelope main document without saving it.

Check Your Work Compare your work to the model answer to ensure that you have completed the activity correctly.

In Addition

Using the Mail Merge Wizard

The Mail Merge feature includes a Mail Merge wizard that guides you through the merge process. To access the Wizard, click the Mailings tab, click the Start Mail Merge button, and then click *Step-by-Step Mail Merge Wizard* at the drop-down list. The first of six Mail Merge task panes displays at the right side of the screen. Complete tasks at one pane and then display the next task pane. The options in each task pane may vary depending on the type of merge you are performing.

A data source file may need editing on a periodic basis to add or delete customer names, update fields, insert new fields, or delete existing fields. To edit a data source file, select the file using the Select Recipients button on the Mailings tab. With the data source file connected to the main document, click the Edit Recipients List button in the Start Mail Merge group. At the Mail Merge Recipients dialog box, click the data source file name in the *Data Source* list box and then click the Edit button. This displays the Edit Data Source dialog box with options for editing, adding, or deleting entries.

What You Will Do　The data source file needs updating to reflect customer changes. You will edit the data source file by deleting an entry, adding a new entry, and changing the last name of an existing customer.

Editing a Data
Source File

1 Open **4-FCTCruiseLtrMainDoc.docx**. (If a message displays asking if you want the document to run the SQL command, click No.)

2 Click the Mailings tab, click the Select Recipients button, and then click *Use an Existing List* at the drop-down list.

3 At the Select Data Source dialog box, navigate to the WordS4 folder and then double-click **4-FCTDataSource.mdb**.

　　4-FCTDataSource.mdb is now connected to 4-FCTCruiseLtrMainDoc.docx.

4 Click the Edit Recipient List button 📇 in the Start Mail Merge group.

5 At the Mail Merge Recipients dialog box, click *4-FCTDataSource.mdb* in the *Data Source* list box and then click the Edit button.

6 At the Edit Data Source dialog box, click the square that displays at the beginning of the row for *Mr. and Mrs. Walter Noretto* and then click the Delete Entry button.

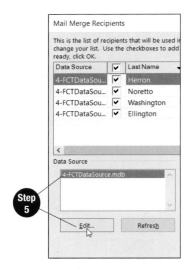
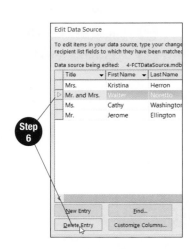

7 At the message that displays asking if you want to delete the entry, click Yes.

In Brief

Edit Data Source
1. Click Mailings tab.
2. Click Select Recipients button.
3. Click *Use an Existing List*.
4. At Select Data Source dialog box, double-click data source file.
5. Click Edit Recipient List button.
6. At Mail Merge Recipients dialog box, click data source file in *Data Source* list box.
7. Click Edit button.
8. Make changes at Edit Data Source dialog box.
9. Click OK.
10. Click Yes.
11. Click OK.

8 Click the New Entry button and then type the following text in the specified fields in the new record:

> Title: Ms.
> First Name: Jane
> Last Name: Goldberg
> Address Line 1: 530 Oak Street
> City: Torrance
> State: CA
> ZIP Code: 90501
> Membership: Premiere Choice
> Discount: 3 percent

9 Kristina Herron has changed her last name. To edit her name, click the last name *Herron* in the *Last Name* column and then type Taylor.

10 Click OK to close the Edit Data Source dialog box.

11 At the message asking if you want to update the recipient list, click Yes.

12 Click OK to close the Mail Merge Recipients dialog box.

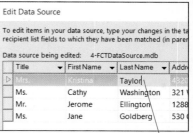

Step 9

13 Click the Merge & Finish button in the Finish group and then click *Edit Individual Documents* at the drop-down list.

14 At the Merge to New Document dialog box, make sure *All* is selected and then click OK.

> The main document is merged with the records in the data source file and a document displays with four merged letters.

15 Save the merged letters in the normal manner and name the document **4-FCTEditedDSLtrs**.

16 Print and then close **4-FCTEditedDSLtrs.docx**.

17 Save and then close **FCTCruiseLtrMainDoc.docx**.

Check Your Work Compare your work to the model answer to ensure that you have completed the activity correctly.

In Addition

Inserting a New Field in a Data Source File

A new field can be inserted in an existing data source file. To do this, display the Edit Data Source dialog box and then click the Customize Columns button. At the Customize Address List dialog box, click the Add button. At the Add Field dialog box, type the name of the new field and then click OK. Click OK to close the Customize Address List dialog box. At the Edit Data Source dialog box, type the desired information in the new field.

Selecting Specific Records

Each record in the Mail Merge Recipients dialog box contains a check mark before the first field. If you want to select specific records for merging, remove the check marks from those records you do not want to include in the merge.

Features Summary

Feature	Ribbon Tab, Group	Button	Option
columns	Layout, Page Setup		
Columns dialog box	Layout, Page Setup		*More Columns*
drop cap	Insert, Text		
Drop Cap dialog box	Insert, Text		*Drop Cap Options*
Insert Address Block dialog box	Mailings, Write & Insert Fields		
insert file	Insert, Text		*Text from File*
Insert Greeting Line dialog box	Mailings, Write & Insert Fields		
Insert Hyperlink dialog box	Insert, Links		
insert merge field	Mailings, Write & Insert Fields		
Insert Table dialog box	Insert, Tables		*Insert Table*
merge documents	Mailings, Finish		
section break (continuous)	Layout, Page Setup		*Continuous*
select recipients	Mailings, Start Mail Merge		
shapes and lines	Insert, Illustrations		
SmartArt	Insert, Illustrations		
start mail merge	Mailings, Start Mail Merge		
table	Insert, Tables		
text box	Insert, Text		
WordArt	Insert, Text		

Workbook Section study tools and assessment activities are available in the *Workbook* ebook. These resources are designed to help you further develop and demonstrate mastery of the skills learned in this section.

INDEX

formatting
  applying styles, 56–57
  changing default, 56–57
  comparing, 45
  default, 5
  finding and replacing, 44–45
  with Font dialog box, 36–37
  with Font Group, 34–35
  with Format Painter, 36–37
  images, 81–83
  inserting
    footers, 72–73
    headers, 72–73
    page numbers, 72–73
  with Mini Toolbar, 34–35
  MLA style, 74–79
  revealing, 45
  tables
    creating, 100–103
    design, 104–105
    layout, 102–103
  with themes, 57, 66–67
Freeform option, 95

G

grammar, checking, 12–13
Grammar task pane, 12, 13
graphics, creating SmartArt
  graphics, 96–99
Greeting Line button, 112

H

hanging indent, 40
hard page break, 71
Header button, 72
headers
  creating own, 73
  described, 72
  inserting, 73–74
  omitting, from first page of
    document, 77
headings
  collapsing and expanding, 57
  creating and modifying using
    WordArt, 90–91
Help
  on buttons, 27
  using, 26–27
Help button, 26
Home key, 9
horizontal ruler, 2, 3
Hyperlink button, 108
hyperlinks
  inserting, 108–109
  in Reveal Formatting task pane,
    45

I

I-beam pointer, 2, 3
images
  downloading and saving from
    Web, 109

drawing shapes, 92, 93–95
  inserting, sizing and moving,
    81–83
indenting text, 40–41
Insert Above button, 101
Insert Citation button, 75, 76
Insert File dialog box, 106
Insert Hyperlink dialog box, 108
inserting
  blank page, 71
  borders, 54–55
  bullets, 46–47
  citations, 74–77
  continuous section breaks, 106
  cover page, 70–71
  footers, 72–73
  headers, 72–73
  images, 81–83
  numbers within text, 46–47
  page break, 71
  page numbers, 72–73
  section break, 106–107
  special characters, 48–49
  symbols, 48–49
  text, 8–9
insertion point, 2, 3
  moving, 8–9
  moving between cells in table,
    100
  resuming reading or editing
    document, 11
Insert Left button, 101
Insert Merge Field button, 112
Insert Right button, 101
Insert Table dialog box, 103
Italic button, 34

J

Justify button, 38

K

Keep Source Formatting button, 62
keyboard shortcuts
  aligning text, 39
  display/hide ribbon, 21
  font, 37
  indenting text, 41
  inserting symbols/special
    characters, 49
  insertion point, 9
  repeat a command, 36
  selecting cells, 103
  tables, 103

L

Label Options dialog box, 86, 87
labels
  customizing, 87
  preparing mailing, 86–87
Labels button, 86
landscape orientation, 67
Larger button, 99

Layout Options button, 83
leaders, setting tabs with, 52–53
left tab symbol, 50
letterheads, creating and modifying
  using WordArt, 90–91
letter template, 28–29
Line and Paragraph Spacing
  button, 42
lines
  border lines in tables, 104–105
  default spacing, 42, 56, 57
  drawing, 95
  No Spacing style, 57
  spacing changes, 42–43, 57
lists, creating numbered/bulleted,
  46–47
live preview, 35

M

mailing labels, preparing, 86–87
mail merge, 110–113
  selecting specific records, 115
Mail Merge wizard, 113
main document, 110
margins, changing page, 66–67
Margins button, 66
Merge Cells button, 101
Merge Formatting button, 62, 63
Mini toolbar, applying formatting to
  documents using, 34–35
MLA (Modern Language
  Association) Style
  formatting, 74–79
  formatting first page of, 77
  general guidelines, 74
  work cited guidelines, 79
monospaced type, 35
More button, 23
More Shape Styles button, 93
mouse
  moving and copying text with, 63
  selecting text with, 10–11
Multiple Page button, 18

N

navigating in document, 10–11,
  20
Navigation Pane
  displaying, 20
  navigating and finding text,
    20–21
  using, 20–21
New Address List dialog box,
  110–111
New option, 5
newspaper columns, creating and
  modifying, 106–107
New Window button, 19
Next button, 16
Next Search Result button, 21
Normal template, 28

No Spacing style, 57
Numbering button, 46
numbers/numbering
  inserting page, 72–73
  inserting within text, 46–47
  turning off automatic, 47

O

Object button arrow, 106
OneDrive-Personal option, 4
100% button, 18
One Page button, 18
Online Pictures button, 81
online templates, 28, 29
Open backstage area, 8
opening
  document, 8–9
  Word, 2
Open option, 5, 8
Options option, 5
organizational charts, using
  SmartArt graphics, 96–99
orientation, changing page, 66–67
Orientation button, 66

P

Page Borders button, 68
Page Break button, 71
Page Color button, 68
Page Number button, 72, 107
pages
  customizing
    color and background, 68–69
    setup, 66–67
  default setting, 66
  inserting
    blank or cover page, 70–71
    numbers, 72–73
    page break, 71
  orientation, 66–67
  printing range, 27
Pages tab, 20
paragraphs
  aligning changes, 38–39
  default alignment, 38
  default spacing, 56, 57
  indenting, 40–41
  numbering, 46–47
  spacing above or below, 43
  spacing changes, 42–43, 57
Paragraph Spacing button, 56
Paste button, 62
Paste Options button, 62
Paste Special dialog box, 63
pasting text, 62–65
PDF file
  described, 108
  editing, 31
  saving as, 108–109
Picture Effects button, 82
Pictures button, 82